How to

WRITE GREAT COPY

Learn the unwritten
Rules of Copywriting

Second edition

Dominic Gettins

KOGAN PAGE

London and Philadelphia

First published in 2000 as *The Unwritten Rules of Copywriting*
Second edition published in 2006 as *How to Write Great Copy*
Reprinted 2007, 2008

Kogan Page Limited
120 Pentonville Road
London N1 9JN
United Kingdom
www.koganpage.com

Kogan Page US
525 South 4th Street, #241
Philadelphia PA 19147
USA

© Dominic Gettins, 2000, 2006

ISBN-10   0 7494 4663 3
ISBN-13   978 0 7494 4663 5

British Library Cataloguing in Publication Data

A CIP record for this book is available from the British Library.

Library of Congress Cataloging-in-Publication Data

Gettins, Dominic.
   How to write great copy : learn the unwritten rules of copywriting / Dominic Gettins.—2nd ed.
      p. cm.
   ISBN 0-7494-4663-3
   1. Advertising copy—Handbooks, manuals, etc. I. Title.
HF5825.G45 2006
659.13'2—dc22
                                                2005035378

Typeset by Saxon Graphics Ltd, Derby
Printed and bound in India by Replika Press Pvt Ltd

CREDITS

Stella: 'Chair'
Creative team: Andy Amadeo, Mick Mahoney,
Photo: Jenny Van Sommers, Type: Andy Amadeo,
Mick Mahoney, Marketing Exec: Stuart McFarlane,
Client: Stella Artois

Stella: 'Moped'
Creative team: Andy Amadeo, Mick Mahoney,
Photo: Jenny Van Sommers, Type: Andy Amadeo,
Mick Mahoney, Marketing Exec: Stuart McFarlane,
Client: Stella Artois

Stella: 'Table'
Creative team: Andy Amadeo, Mick Mahoney,
Photo: Jenny Van Sommers, Type: Andy Amadeo,
Mick Mahoney, Marketing Exec: Stuart McFarlane,
Client: Stella Artois

Volvo: ' If the welding isn't strong enough…'
AD: Ron Brown, Copy: David Abbott, Photo: Martin
Thompson, Type: Joe Hoza, Agency: Abbot Mead
Vickers, Marketing Director: Bill Phelan, Client: Volvo
1985

Tampax: 'You know those irritating ads…'
AD: Damon Collins, Copy: Mary Wear, Illustrator:
Damon Collins, Type: Neil Craddock, Damon Collins,
Creative Director: David Abbott, Agency: Abbott Mead
Vickers, Account Handlers: Monica Middleton, Rachel
Moore, Marketing Exec: Michelle Jobling, Client:
Tambrands

Tampax: 'Easily embarrassed…?'
AD: Damon Collins, Copy: Mary Wear, Ill: Damon
Collins, Type: Neil Craddock, Damon Collins, Creative
Director: David Abbott, Agency: Abbott Mead Vickers
BBDO, Account Handlers: Monica Middleton, Rachel
Moore, Marketing Exec: Michelle Jobling, Client:
Tambrands

The Economist: 'Plankton, Game show host…'
AD: Paul Briganshaw, Copy: Malcolm Duffy, Type: Joe
Hoza, Agency: Abbott Mead Vickers BBDO, Marketing
Manager: Chantal Hughes, Client: The Economist

The Economist: 'Bus – high office'
AD: Paul Briganshaw, Copy: Malcolm Duffy, David
Abbott, Photographer: Neil Evans, Type: Joe Hoza,
Agency: Abbott Mead Vickers BBDO, Circulation
Manager: Chris Collins, Client: The Economist

K Shoes: 'The tights weigh more than the shoe'
AD: Russell Ramsey, Copy: John O'Keefe, Photo:
Andreas Heumann, Type: Mathew Kemsley, Agency:
Bartle Bogle Hegarty, Senior Director: David Rist,
Client: K Shoemakers Ltd

Windsor Healthcare: 'If your skin was…'
AD: Paul Shearer, Copy: Rob Jack, Mike Rix, Agency:
Butterfield Day Devito Hockney, Marketing Manager:
Andrew Dixon, Client: Windsor Healthcare

Wallis: 'Dress to Kill'
AD/CW: Steve Hudson, Victoria Fallon, Photo: Bob
Carlos-Clarke, Type: Andy Bird, Creative Directors:
Bruce Crouch, Graham Watson, Agency: Bartle Bogle

Hegarty, Account Handler: Shazia Brawley, Marketing
Exec: Fiona Davis, Client: Wallis

VW: 'Do we drive our mechanics too hard?'
AD: Mark Reddy, Copy: Tony Cox, Photo: Andreas
Heumann, Type: David Wakefield, Agency: BMP DDB
Needham, VW and Audi Ad Manager: John Mezaros,
Client: VAG (UK) Ltd

Volvo: 'Side Impact Protection System'
AD: Paul Brazier, CW: Peter Souter, Director: Paul
Weiland, Producer: Kate Taylor, Creative Director:
David Abbott, Account Director: Chris Thomas, Client:
Volvo

Ball Partnership: 'There is a spelling mistake…'
AD: Neil French, CW: Neil French, Agency: The Ball
Partnership, Client: The Ball Partnership

Nursing: 'Cockroaches'
AD: John Messum, Colin Jones, Copy: Mike McKenna,
Photo: Graham Cornthwaite, Type: Roger Kennedy,
Creative Directors: Adam Kean, Alexandra Taylor,
Agency: Saatchi & Saatchi, Account Handler: Norma
Clarke, Marketing Exec: Romola Christopherson, Jan
Carver, Client: Dept of Health/COI

Stella: 'My shout, he whispered'
AD: Ken Hoggins, Copy: Chris O'Shea, Photo: Bryce
Attwell, Type: Brian Hill, Agency: Lowe-Howard Spink
Marshalk Ltd, Marketing Director: Peter Bell, Client:
Whitbread & Co Ltd

Volvo: 'How to improve a Golf's turning circle'
AD: Mark Roalfe, Copy: Robert Campbell, Photo: Jerry
Oke, Type: Joe Hoza, Agency: Abbott Mead Vickers
BBDO, Marketing Manager: Oliver Johnson, Client:
Volvo Concessionaires

Wayne McLaren: 'Anti smoking ad'
AD David Gardiner, Pete Favat, Copy: Stu Cooperrider,
Type: Aryn Anderson, Creative Directors: Rich Herstek,
Pete Favat, Agency: Houston Herstek Favat, Account
Handler: Anne Miller, Marketing Exec: Greg Connolly,
Client: Massachusetts Dept of Health

Subdue: 'It works better…'
AD: Joe Ivey, Copy: Scott Crawford, Photo: Steve
Bronstein, Agency: Howard Merrell & Partners, Client:
Ciba-Geigy Turf and Ornamentals

Mercedes: 'Skidmarks'
AD: Marl Tutssel, CW: Nick Bell, Photo: Russell Porcas,
Type: Trevor Slabber, Creative Director: Gerard Stamp,
Agency: Leo Burnetts, Account Handler: Crispin Reed,
Marketing Exec: Oliver Johnson, Client: Mercedes-Benz

Adelar Obedience Training: 'Dog'
AD: Dean Mortensen, Copy: Simon Mainwaring, Photo:
Alister Clarke, Agency: DDB Needham Sydney,
Marketing Exec: Peter Farrelly-Rogers, Client: Adelar
Obedience Training

The Economist: 'Blunt yet sharp'
AD: Malcolm Duffy, Copy: Paul Briganshaw, Type:
Joe Hoza, Creative Director: David Abbot, Agency:

Credits

Abbott Mead Vickers BBDO, Account Director: Jeremy Miles, Client: The Economist

Chick-Fil-A: 'Cows on poster'
AD: David Ring, Copy: Gail Barlow, Creative Director: Gary Gibson, Doug Rucker, Sculptor: Jerry Small, Agency: The Richards Group, Client: Chick-Fil-A

Saigon Restaurant: 'To get better Vietnamese food than mine...'
AD: Bob Marberry, Copy: Dick Thomas, Photo: Rick Dublin, Agency: Bobco/Mpls Client: The Saigon Restaurant

BB2 Idents (various)
Graphic Designers: Brendon Norman-Ross, Sue Worthy, Maylin Lee, Directors: Brendon Norman-Ross, Sue Worthy, Maylin Lee, Model Makers: Asylum Model Makers, Artem Model Makers, Music: Logarhythm, Lighting Cam: Doug Foster, George Theophanous, Harry Op, Rob Harvey, Mike McGee, Production Co: BBC Presentation TV, Client: BBC Presentation

Edward Scissorhands
AD: Lynn Kendrick, Copy: David Shane, Photo: Russell Porcas, Type: Lynn Kendrick, Agency: Chiat Day, Managing Director: Fran Minogue, Client: Neutrogena UK Ltd

Texas: 'Pay half now and nothing later'
AD: Gary Marshall, Copy: Paul Marshall, Photo: John Claridge, Type: Jeff Lewis Agency: Leagas Delaney, Marketing Director: Clive Roylance, Client: Texas Homecare

'I just give people what they want. Phenomenal cow sex at a fair price'
AD: Steve Stone, Copy: Bob Kerstetter, Ill: Bob Kerstetter, Agency: Goodby, Berlin and Silverstein, Marketing Exec: Judy Canter, Client: Judy Canter Veterinarian

'Dodgy Brakes?'
AD: Julie Hill, Copy: Mark Waldron, Type: Alex Manolatos, Prop: Peter Johnson, Client: Station Garage

Adidas: 'Just to the sign post'
AD: Dave Dye, Copy: Dave Dye, Photo: The Douglas Brothers, Agency: Leagus Delaney, Marketing Exec: Juliet Melstrom, Client: Adidas

BA: Shuttle 'Yoyo'
AD: Glenn Gibbins, Copy: Simon Roseblade, Tony Barry, Photo: David Gill, Creative Directors: Simon Dicketts, James Lowther, Agency: M&C Saatchi, Account Director: Richard Alford, Marketing Exec: Derek Dear, Jill Manaton, Client: British Airways

BA: Shuttle 'Lift'
AD: Glenn Gibbins, Copy: Simon Roseblade, Tony Barry, Photo: David Gill, Creative Directors: Simon Dicketts, James Lowther, Agency: M&C Saatchi, Account Director: Richard Alford, Marketing Exec: Derek Dear, Jill Manaton, Client: British Airways

Riverside Chocolate Factory: 'No one went to their deathbeds...'
AD: Barton Landsman, Copy: Amy Krouse Rosenthal, Agency: Boy & Girl Advertising/Chicago, Client: Riverside Chocolate Factory

Peugeot: 'Splash'
AD: Andy Bunday, Copy: John Lilley, Photo: Kevin Griffin, Type: Micky Tonello, Creative Director: Mark Wnek, Agency: Euro RSCG Wnek Gosper, Marketing Director: Kel Walker, Client: Peugeot

United Colors of Benetton: 'Priest and nun kissing'
Concept/Photo: Oliviera Toscani, Creative Director: Oliviera Toscani, Client: Benetton

Conservative Party: 'Hospitals'
CW: Mick Foden, Type: Justin Shill, CD: Alan Jarvie, Agency: IS, Client: The Conservative Party

Coca Cola: 'Love'
Agency: Mother, Client: Coca Cola

Playstation: 'Finger'
AD/Ill: Gareth Lessing, CW: Benjamin Abramowitz, Photo: Clive Stewart, CD: Frances Luckin, Sandra de Witt, Agency: TBWA Hunt Lascaris, AH: Bridget Booms, M Exec: Sue Cockroft, Client: Sony

Merrydown Cider: 'Faces'
AD: Dave Dye, CW: Sean Doyle, Ill: Paul Davies/Fiona Hewitt/Greg Clarke/Jonny Hannah, Type: Dave Dye, CD: Dave Dye, Sean Doyle, Agency: Campbell Doyle Dye, AC: Caspar Thykier/Erica Maran, Brand Manager: Chris Carr

COI: 'If you smoke, I smoke'
AD: Matt Doman, CW: Ian Heartfield, Type: Mark Elwood, Ill: Barnaby, CD: Paul Belford, Nigel Roberts, Agency: AMV BBDO, AH: Cecile Beaufils, Account Manager: Jeeve Gupta, Client: DoH/COI

Adnams: 'Coast'
AD: Dave Dye, CW: Sean Doyle, Ill: Chris Wormell, Type: Dave Wakefield, CD: Dave Dye, Sean Doyle, Agency: Campbell Doyle Dye, AH: Monica Taylor, Marketing Manager: Andy Wood, Brand Manager: Simon Loftus, Client: Adnams

Remington
AD: Jonathan Marlow, CW: Jimmy Blom, Photo: Alan Clarke, Type: Andy Dymock, CD: David Alberts, Project Manager: Rhys Chapman, Art Buyer: Julie Hughes, Agency: Grey London, AH: Liz Addis, Brand Manager: Kay Downs, Client: Remington

Miel: 'Our Pastries'
AD: Holly Fiss, CW: Terese Zeccardi, Photo: Steve Hone, Agency: Tierney Communications Philadelphia, Client: Miel Patisserie

Yamaha: 'Trumpet/Guitar'
AD: Stefan Leick, Raphael Puttman, CW: Stephan Deisenhofer, Mario Gamper, Photo: Piet Truhlar, Agency: Scholz & Friends Berlin, Client: Yamaha

Honda
CW: Ben Walker/Sean Thompson/Tony Chancellor/John Cherry/Matt Giooden, CD: Tony Davidson/Kim Papworth, Agency: Weiden & Kennedy UK, AD: Francesca Birch Group Account Director, Director: Jonathan Campbell, Marketing Manager: Matt Coombe, Client: Honda UK

Olympus: 'Bike lock'
AD: Matt Hazel, CW: Jane Atkinson, CD: Malcolm Poynton, Producer: Trish Burgo, Agency: Saatchi & Saatchi Sydney, AH: Paul Mendham, Marketing Manager: Bill Andreas, Client: Olympus Australia

Ben and Jerry's: 'Granny-like generosity/chunks/ingredients we reserve, imprecision'
AD: Dave Masterman, Andy Johns, CW: Ed Edwards, John Cross, Ill: James Townsend, Type: James Townsend, CD: Richard Flintham, Andy McLeod, Agency: Fallon London, AH: Charlie Hurrell, Marketing Director: Helen Jones

British Heart Foundation: 'Artery'
AD: Philip Beaumont, CW: Samantha Richards, CD: Nick Hastings, Photo: Mike Parsons, Type: Mark Osborne, Account Director: Simon Toaldo, Agency: Euro RSCG London, Client: Colin Gruar (Head of Marketing)

Pilsner Urquell: 'Ditty'
AD: Dexter Ginn, CW: Dominic Gettins, Type: Dave Jenner, Dexter Ginn, Photo: Dave Preutz, Agency: Euro RSCG London, Marketing Exec: Julian Spooner, Client: Guinness

COI: 'doll'
AD: Dave Prater, CW: Imran Patel, Type: Matt Palmer, Photo: Jonathan Kitchen, Account Handler: Merry-Scott Jones, Agency: Euro RSCG London, Client: ODPM

Citroen C1: 'Giraffe'
AD: Steve Nicholls/Matthew Anderson, CW: Steve Nicholls/Matthew Anderson, CD: Justin Hooper, Photo: Nick Meek, Type: Mark Osborne, Account Manager: Patrick Armitage, Account Director: Harriett Elliott, Agency: Euro RSCG London, Marketing Director: Mike Ibbett

Peugeot 206: 'toast'
AD: Olly Caporn, CW: Dominic Gettins, CD: Mark Wnek, Type: Mark Cakebread, Photo: Jenny van Sommers, AH: Nick McElwee, Agency: Euro RSCG London, Marketing Exec: Rod Philpot, Client: Peugeot

ACKNOWLEDGEMENTS

To those kind individuals who attained permissions and artwork on my behalf, especially Moreyba Bidessie. Special thanks to Gerry, Kirsty and Kirsty.

CONTENTS

Contents

FOREWORD

I think it was Gibb the Younger who said, 'It's only words but words are all I have to take your heart away.'

Words were certainly all I had when asked earlier this year to take the stand at Unilever House and address a body of men and women who call themselves '26'. So called after the number of letters in the alphabet, 26 is made up of people who write for a living. Otherwise they look and act like perfectly normal human beings.

My invitation to speak was part of an outreach programme 26 are running toward commercial writers from different disciplines. DDB's Will Awdrey and Radio's own Paul Burke stood alongside me to try to explain what an advertising writer actually does. Well, there's precious little writing for a start. In almost 30 years as a copywriter I don't suppose I've had more than a couple of thousand words broadcast or published. Copywriter is as redundant a job title as haberdasher; indeed, increasingly there's less and less haber to dash. The *nomenclature de nos jours* is 'creative'. This particular 'C' word first started being used as a noun in the early 1980s. I still hate it. It's lazy. 'Creative' covers almost every human endeavour, from the writing of *King Lear* to the making of drinks coasters from stale digestive biscuits and a coat of yacht varnish.

What we really do is conceptualize. We take the base commercial desires of our clients and fashion them into ideas that 'resonate' (a buzz word in every sense) with consumers. Subsequently that idea may need to be expressed in print, radio, online or television, or whatever the most appropriate medium might be. That might involve some actual writing. For me the real creative work lies in taking those sometimes complex marketing objectives and distilling them down to a simple communicable idea that can change attitudes and, ultimately, behaviour. The concept behind the Nike brand, for example, is 'irreverence justified'. Two words worth about a billion dollars each. Together they make Nike a brand and not just a shoe. Those two little words inform all of Nike's communications, from the ads they run to the people they hire to the stars they choose to sponsor. Any self-respecting street kid can tell you the difference between Nike and Adidas. The shoes may be interchangeable but the brands are distinct. That's what we do: we create those differences and make them worth something. Everything else is subservient to that objective.

Someone once suggested the title 'concepteur' to describe our primary function. Obviously this sounds hopelessly French and pretentious. It reminds me that the most famous of all French copywriters, Jacques Seguela, called his autobiography, *Don't Tell My Mother I Work in Advertising, She Thinks I Play Piano in a Brothel*. This tells us a lot about French intellectual snobbery and the sexual mores of the bourgeoisie but is no help in providing us with a modern and relevant job descriptor. I only think it's important because I sense there's a ceding of the high ground by today's creative thinkers from having big ideas to just making ads. I'm certainly not demeaning the latter skill-set but if that's really our sole *raison d'etre* then perhaps we should be working for production companies not advertising agencies. But I digress; a funny thing happened to me on my way to this 26 gig.

Whenever you're put in a position of having to explain what you do to people who are not 'in the life', you inevitably start to regain some objectivity toward your job function. This reappraisal was made all the more poignant for me by watching my son take his first faltering steps as a copywriter. He's decided to take up the Moira baton and let's hope he'll be shoving it up an account man near you in the near future. But what kind of future will it be? I don't think the business of writing in advertising has ever been under such intense pressure. First, you have the established tectonic plates of Compression and Abstraction. These two, often conflicting, forces are rubbing against each other with more friction than ever before. Compressing the global ambitions of giant conglomerates into 30 seconds has never been as easy as it looked. Now, any self-respecting CEO wants to see his corporate face reflected in an online banner! The ad-byte is with us and the USP is no longer. Compression was a relatively simple exercise when you could reduce it to simple product superiority. Creating a differentiated brand personality takes longer. Barclays (or any other High Street bank) has long since abandoned any pretence to a 'better mouse trap', but they've got Samuel L Jackson and your bank hasn't... hah! It's no wonder that cliché, parody and celebrity endorsement are the copywriter's best friends. There's no time and less and less media money for character development, a back story or second act in contemporary TV campaigns. Imagine the cost of establishing a Heineken or Hamlet at today's rate of media inflation and audience fragmentation.

If Compression is about reducing our clients' offering to its most condensed and compelling expression, then Abstraction is about acknowledging that nobody else gives a damn.

Nobody pays their Sky subscription or TV licence to watch the ads. We have to make things interesting. And in setting out one's stall it's no longer enough to give the apples a good polish. These days you have to pose naked with a banana and a couple of kiwi fruit to raise an eyebrow, let alone anything more substantial. We have to create new news and the quest for novelty almost inevitably takes us further and further away from our overt purpose. The average UK citizen receives around 3,000 advertising hits each day. By the time the average Brit reaches his or her 35th birthday, she or he will have already seen 150,000 commercials. What space do your efforts occupy in their over-loaded, over-stimulated memory banks? In the struggle for cut-through, the word is that words are no longer up to the job.

There are only three kinds of word-dependent TV advertising left. There's the old Persuasion Model from advertising's Jurassic period. This is still used by the P&G's, L'Oreals and 'better mouse trap' people who believe that 30 seconds of rational argument can affect behaviour change. Sharks are from the Jurassic period too and they've survived because they're efficient. This model must work for those with sufficient NPD programmes to support it.

Next you have that rare visitor to our shores, The Corporate Philosopher. Really a US native, this 'let's talk about us' approach has failed to find popularity or talented practitioners here, early Orange work and the Honda OK spot being the exceptions. Last, there's the overwhelming British favourite, The Sponsored Sketch. Invented by CDP in the 1970s, refined by BMP in the 1980s and then roughed-up a bit by HHCL in the 1990s, The Sponsored Sketch has become the preferred form of expression for most UK copywriters. This is their last redoubt against the serried ranks of art college clones, of post-production trickery, MTV cliché and minimalist cool. Not to mention some of the most reductive and conformist research techniques ever devised by man to squeeze life and individuality out of an idea.

We've come a long way since the Abbott/Hegarty Arts and Crafts Movement of the early 1980s. There's a New Brutalism about that argues that making good TV ads is a purely instinctive process like producing good rock 'n' roll. It's all about feel and texture and image, man. The New Brutalists are suspicious of words; they believe brainy, articulate people should be confined to the Planning Department. But the truth is that words have never been cooler. Britons buy more newspapers than any other nation. We read more books than any other nation. Indeed, book sales rose by over 40 per cent from 1997 to 2001. Radio 4 is one of the great media success stories of the last five years. Words are still the best medium for the expression of ideas and Maurice Gibb was right about their unique emotional power. The question is, are our writers up to the challenge?

Gerry Moira
Head of Creativity, EuroRSCG London

INTRODUCTION

Afresh, afresh, afresh.
Philip Larkin

While people who write about marketing usually get on with it fairly sensibly, those who write about creativity often employ the uplifting style and circular logic of creationist pastors. They look upon an end product and decide that it is so perfect and beautiful that it could only have come about by divine inspiration. They then set about inspiring you. They show you a Honda commercial or VW's break-dancing Gene Kelly and say it is a thing of wonder and that you too can produce such wonders if only you'd let yourself be inspired. This book aspires to be different in that respect. It is written not by a guru, nor a president of a global corporation, but by someone who writes ads and witnesses on a daily basis what human beings go through to produce their best work.

For a start, reverence for creativity is unnecessary. Advertising and marketing are increasingly processes on the same thinking continuum, so just as clients are able to talk comfortably about creativity, creative people are able to talk in detail about brands and markets without constant reminders to push the boundaries and think outside an imaginary box, however much it may amuse.

Inspiration is a lovely thing, but for me it is right up there with cuddles, skids and the hot air blowers above the doors in Marks and Spencer as pleasant, but short-lived sensations.

It is helpful to read an inspirational magazine or a coffee table book displaying the joys of creativity. To see great ads is an education and a very important part of knowing what the industry is about. But the point of a finished ad is to spring everything of importance on you in a compact manner that, like a punch in the face, requires no footnotes. What it isn't designed to do is give you clues as to how it was produced.

I have never been inspired to write good copy by a pep talk or a speech on 'Creativity in the 21st century'. Where something good happens it happens after a digestive process of mundane facts, opinions and knowledge.

Now and then a visiting global chairman will break the low hum of industry to gather everyone in the organization into a conference venue and badger them with talk of rule breaking, anarchy and a constant will to challenge the world order.

But after the downward jet of hot air we are all back on the cold streets and returning to the quotidian dilemmas involved in generating, refining, presenting and producing creative advertising ideas, a process that is, as anyone who contributes will testify, actually conducted in straightforward, problem-solving language, as one would use when designing a washing machine or planning an ascent of a mountain.

Even the most unorthodox of ideas are the product of a slow-moving train of logic. A link between the consumer and the product, an insight into the market that forms a germ of truth that gathers speed in execution toward something original. The anarchistic appearance of, say, a Virgin mobile promotion, is clearly not evidence of an unruly, balaclava'd faction inside the organization, but of a sober decision reached round a table in an office. The spray-can typeface is not a display of defiance by a wild creative but another cog in the cumulative logic in a market where you must get noticed, pinpoint your audience, build a brand.

When I visited the publisher of this book for the first time, I saw on a display of sister publications one called something like *Managing a Small Wood*. Unexpected company to be in, but in a way, appropriate. A tree is a wondrous thing but telling it so doesn't achieve a great deal. Likewise an idea can be powerful, and successful, but the processes of nurturing one is, let's face it, a kind of job. People who make ads know all too well the desired end and need only some unspectacular detail on how to get there. This can come from experience, a course, or from a practical resource book like this one.

It may be a calumny to suggest to a marketing guru that communications in all their profundity and complexity are to be compared to tree surgery. When Jean-Marie Dru, president and CEO of TBWA Worldwide writes about the industry he talks not of practicalities but seemingly of the most exciting challenge facing humanity. Headings in his book, *Disruption* read as though they were splitting apart the fabric of the universe. 'Disruption at the premium nexus' and 'The Tyranny of Or' feel a long way away from what I do for a living. Does a task as simple as selling a product really need these paroxysms of abstract expression? Why isn't the manager of a small wood asked to think beyond sap, or question the tyranny of coppicing?

The substance of copywriting is indeed mundane. Most of us learn it unwittingly at school under the guise of English lessons. Most low-level, intra-departmental creative chats really are about pruning and chopping (appropriately enough) enlivened with obedience to certain unspoken rules: say one thing and one thing only. Use six words or less. Don't say in a headline what you show in a picture. Don't pun. Show the positive not the negative. Laws of layout, laws of presentation, laws of strategy, laws of logic.

These rules are already there in agencies and in marketing departments, but they are unwritten, passed on in the same way that Bushmen pass on how to carve wooden neck-rests or Mongolian herdsmen pass on best practice in the matter of skinning reindeer. By word of mouth, or by example.

I mean, how hard is it to keep a hospital clean?

ARE YOU THINKING WHAT WE'RE THINKING?

CONSERVATIVE

The point of formalizing the rules in chapter headings and lists is simply to make them easier to remember, rendering them instantly more useful to everyone involved. Especially as even the most experienced practitioner can overlook the basics.

Lord Saatchi confessed to transgressing one of his own rules during the 2005 Conservative Party election campaign. His may be the greatest surname in advertising, but there he was, quoted in *The Guardian* (20 June 2005) saying that by not creating a consumer benefit in that campaign, by only pointing at dirty hospitals and immigration problems, the campaign had failed. The campaign was excellent in many other ways, indeed a nostalgic visit to old-skool Saatchi & Saatchi. Beautifully simple art direction of unarguable propositions. But it carried no consumer benefit, nor even implied one. The pay off to the ads was the line 'Are you thinking what we're thinking?' It is one of the oddities of the advertising industry that such a slip can be made by the best of us, while the layman called upon to advertise rarely overlooks such basics. My local retailer of domestic fish tanks instinctively knows to offer a product benefit in its window sticker: 'Calm down with an aquarium.'

By contrast the Labour Party campaign that year was anything but textbook in execution. The posters I think were generally poor; most have vanished from the public memory and it would be unfriendly to dig them out. But strategically the advertising stuck to a fundamental rule understood by sellers of aquaria the world over, by offering a positive benefit.

Forward not back. It seems a very average line and probably had Conservative strategists giggling uncontrollably. But it's deceptive. The unfussy language and controlled determination set the right tone for a party that was otherwise in bother.

Skipping the rule about selling positive benefits is a blunder, but you might wonder at my gall when there is no rule about selling benefits in this book. There are two reasons 'Be positive' isn't here. The first is that not all communication is selling.

Selling the benefits doesn't always help if you are charged with making a charity ad, for example, or one that is trying to shame people into giving up smoking. A selling benefit is the raw material that a creative team is given by the planning department or in the original brief from the client. If the job of writing ads were merely to enthuse about every product one is handed, this book would be very short. (That's not to say I haven't met quite a few in advertising who actually think this is their function.)

Secondly, 'Be positive' belongs in an inspirational book, where it would take its place alongside headings such as 'Think outside the box', 'Push the envelope', 'Go the extra mile'. These rules you can write for yourself. In fact, since you have started to read this book you will probably find you already have them in place. Such thoughts are constantly in the minds of those self-starting, highly motivated individuals that wash up in advertising agencies and marketing departments.

But where selling something *is* the goal, of course, be positive. It goes without saying. In the early days of commercial TV in the UK it was commonplace for people to say that the ads were better than the programmes. It was true in the superficial sense, that commercials that lasted 30 or 60 seconds on which creative minds had slaved for months often had demonstrably more allure than some lesser TV serials. But it was also that in general the message of advertising was so ludicrously upbeat. Nowadays we believe less in the grinning, thumbs up, dancing vegetables form of the genre that was the norm in the 1960s and 70s. But today's car commercials and ring tone download spots are all still predicated on the holding out of aspirations. To quote from a famous US commercial from the 1960s as used in a later chapter of this book:

These are the stakes. To make a world in which all God's children can live. Or to go into the dark. We must either love each other, or we must die.
Lyndon Johnson, Democratic Election TV Commercial, 1964

Now that's how to win an election. It's also, currently, how to sell Coke.

So to go back to Jean-Marie Dru and the question of why mature men and women all over the world get so worked up about the production of advertising. The high blown language and inspirational mottoes may inspire, but the listener is probably more inspired by the speaker's salary than the message. In truth, the accidental role of much advertising is to generate what is to some a culture of greed, but to others a general background of positivity. If nothing else it is at least a reminder that each blank sheet of paper is a chance to produce, like the man who plants trees, one thing that's positive, perfect and original.

THIS GUIDE

The supply of words in the world market is plentiful, but the demand is falling.

Lech Walesa, Newsweek, November 1989

It is a consensus view that this is a visual age and whatever that means and however it happened, it's true there is a certain trend towards fewer words in advertisements. The congested nature of the environment in which advertisements appear means that simple visual ideas are often the most effective and definitely the most talked about.

'The written word is being replaced by communication through images.' So says John Hegarty, co-founder of Bartle Bogle Hegarty, and others in the advertising industry agree with him. The US writer Marty Cooke says, 'We don't have readers anymore. We have thumbers, browsers, window shoppers through printed media.' Steve Henry says, 'Look at the pictures. Nobody reads body copy.' Neil French says, 'Avoid like genital warts the temptation to start writing.'

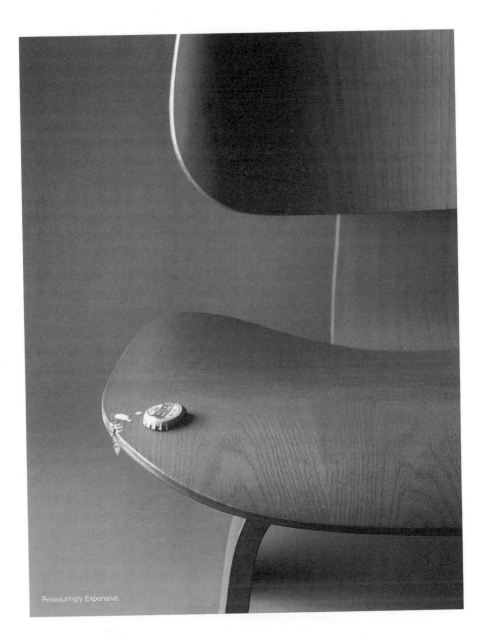

Reassuringly Expensive.

Reassuringly Expensive.

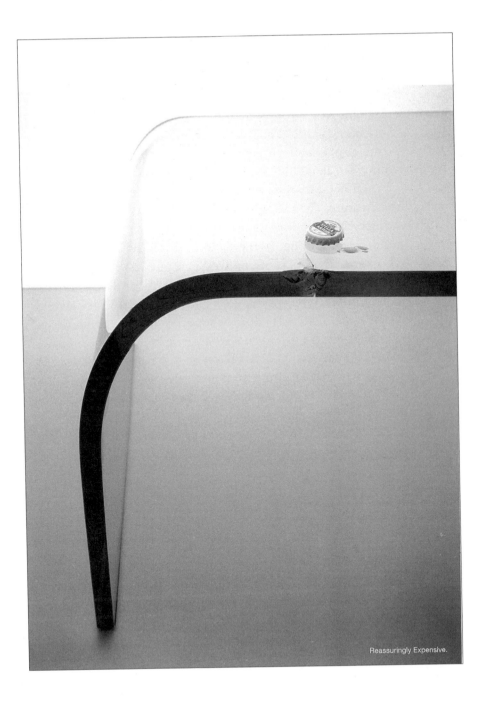

Reassuringly Expensive.

The press ads on pages 9–11 show the benefit of this approach. They are a part of a long-running campaign for Stella Artois, whose endline, 'Reassuringly expensive' was coined in the 1980s. The words today are barely visible on the artwork and you might wonder how the campaign's current writer would justify his existence to a visiting auditor. Fortunately (and here is the theme of this simple guide) the art of writing ads is not about writing, but about thinking.

I hope there is value in this guide for a wide range of occupations. The examples used come from the advertising industry but the techniques may be applied to any form of promotional writing, in the national press, newsletters, press releases, direct mail shots, on websites, posters, TV, radio, even in some cases internal reports and memos. Advertisements tend to be positive, offering solutions not problems; memos should do the same. Good ads improve your day, rather than clutter it; so should direct mail. Even a letter complaining to a company about bad service should make it easy for the respondent to reply if, like an ad, it clearly communicates the desired response.

In general, the standards set are geared towards practitioners of advertising, the copywriters, art directors and designers working freelance and in agencies or consultancies. These are likely to be the most demanding, so there can be little harm in that.

For such people, guidance in advertising tends to come from a combination of admiring the work of past gurus, flicking through awards annuals and picking up habits on the job. In addition, we might occasionally hear catchphrases such as 'Less is more' or the KISS principle of 'Keep It Simple, Stupid'. There are, admittedly, a few gnomic utterances of this kind in what follows. But there is also detail, on such subjects as sentence forming and what copywriters need to know about the various media they might work in.

The guide is presented in the form of eight copywriting rules. It may seem strange to apply rules to an essentially

creative act, but that is their benefit. Much of what you do when creating is intuitive, yet much of what makes great copy is counter-intuitive. For example, when persuading someone to buy a thing the most natural way is to describe it with glowing adjectives, whereas the most effective approach is to present indisputable facts about it or visual proof.

Before embarking on the rules, there's one general thing to be said.

TIME

It doesn't strictly fit into any list of rules, but time is vital to producing copy for a living, and excellence in general. There is never enough time to raise standards for the logical reason that people set deadlines based on past experience. It follows that if you want to do things better than in the past, you might meet some resistance on timing. So whenever a briefing is given or deadline presents itself, always push the apparent time allowed. Is it for real? Or would it magically increase if it turned out that your work wasn't good enough?

Some people have the natural talent to turn out satisfactory ads in a few minutes, but this can be as much a liability as an asset. Satisfactory advertising, no matter how quickly produced, is not a valuable commodity.

All advertising is in a way an extension of the product. In fact, in some areas such as call-direct services or internet brands, it's the only visible manifestation of the product, so it's unwise to cramp its development.

A great idea takes less than a second to occur, but which second it occurs in can't be known at the outset. Asking for this time is one of those things that seem counter-intuitive. It often seems that your job is about impressing people with your mental ability. About heroically solving problems quickly. An organization might feel the same way. There's a natural urge to have the client pleased with you on a day-to-day basis. But although it's arguably more impressive to score 9/10 for a job completed in five minutes, copywriting is not a gymnastic event where you score marks for difficulty. You're better off using the time available properly to score 10/10. Tony Antin says the same in his book, *Great Print Advertising,* in which he states, 'Great advertising demands not just high marks (9.5, 9.7); it demands perfect marks, straight 10s.'

Unfortunately, attaining straight 10s can take not just weeks, but years of practice and experience. The copywriter Andrew Rutherford once told a client that it might take years to do the perfect ad for his product. The client, who was rather hoping to be in the press by the weekend, was confused and dismayed. The value of the following rules is that they can at least speed up the process by which you write and judge ads. If you run a small company it might help you decide whether to write the ads yourself. Or it could help you recognize quickly where an advertisement isn't working or improve one that is. In the end, good advertising makes everyone's job easier. It defines the essence of a company for staff and customers alike and at the same time, sells its products. Two good reasons, I hope, to read on.

EIGHT COPYWRITING
RULES

An advertising agency is 85 per cent confusion and 15 per cent commission.

Fred Allen, US radio comic, Treadmill to Oblivion 2

1.   Know your target market.
2.   Do research.
3.   Answer the brief.
4.   Be relevant.
5.   Be objective.
6.   Keep it simple.
7.   Know your medium.
8.   Be ambitious.

As intimated earlier, there appears to be some misunderstanding on the nature of rules. The maddening frequency with which creative departments are exhorted to break rules is a source of perplexity to young teams who enter the industry only to have their rule breaking ideas swatted without compunction. When a creative director demands that rules must be broken, he or she usually changes his or her tune faced with a truly rule breaking TV commercial. A script written entirely in an ancient Berber dialect would have anyone reaching for a rulebook, but I have sat in innumerable meetings in which strange but promising ideas are batted back with the reprimand that they are not what the client wants.

'What happened to breaking the rules?' the team is entitled to ask. Funnily enough I have yet to meet a client that didn't want to be presented with work that's fresh and exciting. The difference is that they really mean it. They are the ones paying and whose careers most depend on a campaign's success. But fresh and exciting doesn't mean ridiculous. Presenting a script the client doesn't want is as daft as writing it in an ancient alphabet. If a creative director is to have anything to put before a client besides obedience and expensive dentistry, he or she must be able to tell the difference between fresh and exciting, and fresh and irrelevant.

If a team can ensure that their idea is demonstrably relevant, objective, right for the target market and so on, it is armour plated in its quest to get past the echelons of creative directors, account directors, brand directors, marketing directors and beyond in the international directosphere. So too is the creative team's career armour plated.

I suspect that when people say ads should be rule breaking, what they really mean is ground breaking. In fact, what makes the most difference to the power and cut-through of advertising is the extent or extremes to which it is pushed, rather than its contrariness to conventional wisdom. Tony Kaye's allegedly rule breaking Dunlop commercial, showing a number of unexpected things happening on a road, including a grand piano falling from a bridge, was not, as it was often billed, rule breaking. The illusion was that Tony Kaye the director was breaking rules because he acted outrageously and wore outrageous clothes. But the Dunlop commercial? Rule breaking? No. Many letter writers and industry spokespeople said it had no advertising idea behind it, yet it clearly did.

'Expect the unexpected' stated the endline, clearly presenting an argument that Dunlop tyres were of a standard that offered a driver reassurance, regardless of road conditions. The commercial leading up to the endline was merely a demonstration of these conditions. It was only the extent of the demonstration that caused surprise and simultaneously entertained. The usual images used to make this kind of demonstration are familiar: a deer in the road, a spilled load of melons are but two. In the Dunlop commercial these were simply upgraded to falling piano and spiky-haired man in bondage gear rolling ball bearings across the thoroughfare accompanied by a cool track. This doesn't constitute a rule breaking ad. In terms of the idea itself it doesn't even represent a ground breaking ad. It was simply a good ad, made somewhat extraordinary by the execution.

That all said, it is, of course, possible to break any rule. It's fun, and it can often be a logical thing to do. For example, by running a completely irrelevant commercial you may be cleverly saying something anarchic to a youthful target market. Then again, in a way, that only makes it relevant again to your target market, so it hardly bears further comment. Where unwritten rules are genuinely circumvented it is noticeable that it is best done by those who have internalized them.

When David Abbot suspended a Volvo over his head in order to demonstrate the quality of the car's welding, it was a powerful demonstration. When a creative team later appeared in their own ads for the sheer craziness of it all, the results were embarrassing. Both David Abbot and the team broke an unwritten rule by putting their personal stamp on a client's work, but one had an advertising idea attached to it and the other didn't. As the American copywriter Paul Silverman says, 'Anything brilliant can break any rule.' However, if you aren't sure of the brilliance of your advertising idea, a rule may save you some embarrassment.

Given the existence of certain unwritten rules whether used, ignored, denied or flouted, it cannot hurt to write them down for future reference. These rules are not intended as edicts.

They carry no penalties; they're merely a useful way to structure material and endear it to the memory. These rules have been used by the BBC and on one of Britain's best copywriting courses, without creating a breed of grey-suited creative people who crush free thinking and drink only in moderation. In any case, in deference to those who bridle at rules I have added a final semi-rule, at the end of the eight – be original.

I remember a head of client services whose career path briefly crossed mine some years ago. His office was empty apart from his chair, a table and a single piece of A4 paper stuck to a wall on which were written the words, 'People read what interests them and sometimes it's an ad.'

Despite the fact that the next time I saw him was in a magazine article about what it's like to go from £200,000 a year to living on unemployment benefit, the point he put on his wall is a good one. Whatever you do, you have to interest your target market, or all your hard work is in vain. You must at all costs be noticed.

GETTING NOTICED

Getting noticed, as any guru will tell you, is the entry ticket, the foundation stone, the first principle, the *sine qua non* and the first job of any advertisement. It's a priority. Everybody agrees with this proposition, from the top to the bottom of any organization involved in advertising. Odd, then, that it is also one of the most common battlegrounds in meetings between agencies and clients. Extra facts need to go in, extra words, extra logos, recent awards won. Copy briefs are generated for a 96-sheet poster that motorists drive past at high speed. Requests for extra packs in the corner. Subheads. The postal address. All such additions are conscious decisions made by intelligent human beings to decrease the noticability of the ads to the people they're trying to reach.

Up to around five years ago there was really only one answer to this problem. The agency had to insist on simplicity and win. Nothing but ruthless simplicity had the power to get through the first barriers to comprehension.

As will be demonstrated later, 'Keep it simple, stupid' is still the best weapon in any medium, but there are new weapons, broadly described as New Media. These will be described later, but just as important as the technological ability to target virals, run text votes and create media events is the ability to think differently. And that's just what a lot of successful brand managers are doing.

Buzz

With so many new challenges from internet brands, low cost brands, new markets, new products, new fragmentations within brands and so much general thrashing around for the customer's attention, we seem to have reached a tipping point. So desperate are companies to keep their margins and their brand alive that they have finally been forced to confront the one tool that can do this for them. And it's not advertising.

Mark Hughes makes great play and apparently reasonable wealth from this observation in *Buzzmarketing*. The principle idea is, as the subhead has it, to get people to talk about your stuff. Buzz is what was previously called word-of-mouth, with the difference that buzz is intentional and planned for, where word-of-mouth is accidental. But this difference is a semantic one. Where he gets comedians to dress up in funny costumes and hang round certain venues he says it is to generate buzz, and that this is a new concept. Yet people in daft costumes handing out leaflets is not new to this century, so you can't help wondering how the hamburger costumes of earlier generations differed in intention and effect.

There are many useful nuggets in Hughes's book and website, but you start to realize after a while that what he rails against as ineffective is nothing new. Mediocrity is a waste of money at the best of times. As the degree of advertising congestion in our culture reaches its Mr Creosote moment, mediocrity is a sin, or at least a very large mistake. If advertising isn't getting noticed, a £10 million budget can quickly disappear and be replaced with a sponsorship deal, a viral campaign or a text message sent to teenagers' mobile phones.

Hughes wrote in *Admap* in 2004 how a US retailer carefully funnelled several million dollars into conventional advertising which caused not a blip on their sales. He then recalled Miller Beers' experience of creating a massive and very creative campaign featuring a fund of comedy characters and a 'bevy of babes' without raising their profile in the mind of its target at all. As a punishment he refers to creatives as 'creatives' for the rest of his article. It may indeed be the fault of misplaced faith in 'creative guys' when things don't work, but that would not be consistent with his idea that the medium itself is outdated. The point is, it is not the medium or the personnel that is wrong, it is the mediocrity of both.

I know from my own experience that even a large media spend can disappear in the melee never to be seen again. I too worked on a large client, a bank, which marked a decline in its fortunes some years ago by running a series of ads notionally created by their customers. The commercials were intentionally low key, ordinary feeling, amateurish but charming. It was a nice idea and probably made for a good presentation. But nobody seemed to notice the campaign. Nobody remembers them. This was no small campaign. It consisted of 14 TV commercials, one after the other, aired at prime time to the whiff of several million going up in smoke. I only remember because it was conceived in an office near to the one I worked in at the time and to replace a long-running and resoundingly successful one of my own. (It seems the only thing you can do in such situations is to write a book.)

You see fewer such flops today because the market has changed. Large companies have been forced to realize that being right-headed isn't enough. Today the big, big clients feel they can turn their backs on the big, big agencies and cosy relationships of yore, and focus on the importance of having the big, big idea instead. The big idea might come from a big agency, or a small, three-person outfit, or the German office of a little known European agency, or a single mad Swedish person working in their own post room. The interesting point that Mark Hughes makes is buried deep in his book. It isn't the stunt or taboo breaking idea that is new. Nor is the fact that people will talk about interesting things. The point is that unconventional ideas are more powerful than ever before because:

Technology is accelerating word of mouth.

Mark Hughes, Buzzmarketing, 2005

This is the big difference. Take Michael Mullen's experience at Heinz Europe. While e-mailers around the world cruelly passed on the story of Mr Philips, the highly paid London lawyer who demanded £4 from his secretary Mrs Amner to pay for the removal of a ketchup stain on his suit, Michael Mullen issued a statement offering advice on stain removal. He stated that 'Vinegar diluted with water is an easy home remedy,' and offered that Heinz would foot the dry-cleaning bill. 'Why should Ms Amner pay the price for enjoying the world's favourite ketchup?'

Not astounding wit, maybe, but intelligent and timely it was, and switched on to how the brand can behave in the media space. But where once it would have merited a groan from newspaper editors and been spiked along with other marketing managers' predictable attempts to leap on a bandwagon, this response was published around the world as proof of Heinz's wit, charm, family values, great tasting tomato ketchup, you name it. This was because the story had the chance to blow up, by means of e-mail and tabloid journalism, from a tiny non-event, to a

Watergate-scale international issue on which everyone had a view. The two protagonists had to retire from public life for a few days after having unwittingly entered it. The buzz that Heinz got from their intervention was magnificent and Mark Hughes would do you a great graph to prove the benefit of buzzmarketing on the back of it. The benefit is certainly there, but it comes from the story, the interest, the technology, the authenticity. For the industry professional the point is not that you should throw all you media budget into predictable press releases, but that your creative content needs to compete with such Olympian feats of attention getting. You can do so without necessarily relying on conventional media and agencies, without relying on carefully crafted posters and sterile arguments about logos. Along with simplicity, try topicality, authenticity, credibility, originality, humour. But whatever the medium, don't try mediocrity.

Good service

Another point that Mr Mullen unintentionally makes with his headline-grabbing comments is that anyone can now do the fun bit of a creative idea. One piece of effective communication I take notice of almost every day, as do millions like me, doesn't appear to be very simple in execution, nor is it the result of protracted arguments between a client and its agency. But it works powerfully.

Somewhere in the bowels of London Underground management, someone had a brainwave a year or two ago. The Underground system is, or rather was notoriously unreliable. I travelled on it daily and spent many an empty minute on platforms listening to delays announced over a poor PA system, amid a low chorus of commuter moans and stressed gibbering. The entrance halls were decorated with badly spelt apologies for signalling problems or dark references to industrial action, a person under a train at Mortlake or overrunning engineering works. Customers hated the system, hated the staff, hated going to work, hated London. Starting every day like that, they ended up hating everything, going to Mortlake and compounding the problem for everyone else.

Enter the uncredited employee. Uncredited employee noticed that tourists, who simply turned up for a brief period and used the tube for one-off trips thought it was a wonderful system, even the best underground system in the world. Objectively it really was doing a very good job. It was the size of the operation that meant that there was an awful lot of bad news to report every morning. In the spirit of Harry Beck, designer of the original Underground map, the uncredited employee devised a simple graphic solution. Overnight, in every station, there appeared a chart showing, in the left-hand column, every underground line, and in the right a word or two as to their status. From the first day, perception of the tube has been transmogrified by a graphic presentation of the facts, because of all the dozen or so lines, the abiding yet immediate impression was one of 'good service', with only an occasional and proportionate 'delay'. In the context of the whole picture, one delay wasn't worth moaning about. This might sound trivial, it may not be rewarded, if only because the messages were (and often still are) expressed through felt tip pen rather than type, but the impact, both daily and in general on public perception and on employee morale has to be enormous and representative of what good communications are about.

BACK TO THE RULES

Why are the rules arranged in the above order? The main one is that for some reason, being told the golden rule of this or that walk of life is a nice enough experience, but when you think about it, little practical help. It's difficult to sit in an office with a blank pad or a blinking cursor on your computer and just start being simple, or for that matter, ambitious.

Golden rules, don't forget, are usually bestowed by someone looking backwards, having worked their way up through a design or media career, only then finding the mental space necessary to define the essence of it to themselves. 'Advice' as Baz Lehrmann said, 'is a form of nostalgia'. They are also, usually, people who have a gift for making a vast and complicated situation seem simple. Passing on generalizations may inspire, or it may simply induce an admiration for the person doing the passing on. But it doesn't directly instruct.

For that reason, the eight (and a half) rules are in their logical order for writers as they contemplate starting work. Rather than thinking, 'What can I do that will be really good?' a question that is unlikely to produce a fantastic idea by way of an answer, the first thing to do is fill your head. Accurate, honest and up-to-date information is where the finished product is invisibly roosting.

This explains why the first two rules ('Know your target market' and 'Do research') seem to have so little to do with being creative, talking as they do about investigating things and asking questions. Reading about Rule 3 ('Answer the brief') may encourage the first stirrings of original thought, but this is immediately and satisfyingly crushed by the killjoys of Rules 4 and 5. (If you enjoy finger painting, you'll detest advertising.) Once the rules of relevance and objectivity have inspired the production of something worthwhile, the next two rules kindly point out the futility of being merely worthwhile. The only succour for the human soul can be found in the last chapter, on ambition, and the short word on originality.

For the time being, though, it's back to the beginning. You're faced with a blank piece of paper or a blinking cursor and the need to fill your head.

RULE ONE: KNOW YOUR TARGET MARKET

The consumer is not a moron. She is your wife. You insult her intelligence if you assume that a mere slogan and a few rapid adjectives will persuade her to buy anything.
David Ogilvy, *Confessions of an Advertising Man*, 1963

Your first move when you get a brief is probably not to think about the target market. It's far more likely that you will think rather abstractly about the situation. Then you may continue to think rather abstractly, but no longer about the situation. There's nothing wrong in this, of course. You're unlikely to start investigating the target market just because this book tells you to. Nor will you find in this book any of the other basics of the getting started variety, such as hints on the kind of pencil you might like to use or layout pads that have proved popular down the years. Some hints and tips on the practicalities of getting down to work are undeniably useful, but they are well covered elsewhere. Whatever the brief, I would recommend leaving all pens, layout pads, PCs and Macs alone for as long as possible and simply think, or better still, talk.

WHO ARE YOU TALKING TO?

The first subject to think or talk about is the target market. The first goal is to visualize your audience sufficiently well to be able to address him or her in a natural way. If your target market is 'young people' or 'teenagers' you may be tempted to think of them as a general mass of youth, possibly tainted with your own prejudices or predilections. This may lead you eventually to talk to them in a generalized way, to use a youthful message delivery system such as distressed type, shots of young people doing young things like skateboarding or jumping in the air. This may signal your intention to speak to a certain group of people, but won't single you out from all the other product messages in the area, who use the same tactics.

Pinpoint the people you're talking to. Not just 'young people' or ABC 1 Male Mid Market. That's merely a requirement. Know exactly who your target person is, down to what he or she wears, what he or she does in the evening. If you are working for a company that runs research groups or focus groups to canvas views, try, no matter how unappealing the prospect, to attend one or two. Bob Levinson, a writer who started at Doyle Dane Bernbach in 1959, said: '"Males, 18–34" or "Households above £30,000 pa" are categories worse than useless; they are destructive. You may actually have to enter the Hades of the focus group.'

Research groups of this kind are used to produce data and reports for product development teams and marketing men. They have their advocates and their detractors, but putting that debate to one side, they are a goldmine for writers. The main reason for this is the opportunity they offer to eyeball the target market. In fact, the words used at your briefing suddenly revert to the mumbo jumbo you secretly knew them to be when faced with the actual people themselves. The Playstation ad opposite couldn't exist without understanding the dark fascinations of game players, and for that you surely have to meet up. As a human being you are tuned in to receive signals and information about other human beings when you meet them. All of a sudden

the idea of addressing a group of teenagers in your own synthetic idea of teen-speak seems slightly awkward. Just listen to how people are prepared to talk quite naturally about what they look for, or what they hate about the product you offer. You get a natural feel for what they find funny, what they notice, their everyday terminology and probably hundreds of subtle things that needn't go into a report, but will be somewhere useful in your brain when it comes to addressing the group in advertising terms.

Take these Tampax ads, for example. What's pleasant about this work is that there's nothing false about it. It talks to teenage girls about a sensitive issue, in a way that those teenage girls are unlikely to reject. This isn't just important for getting the information across. That could be achieved with almost any style of advertising for the simple reason that teenage girls are hungry for this information. It appears in a safe environment – the teenage press that they buy with their own money and read privately in their own bedrooms. So, even if the information had been expressed in a crass fashion, with a young model leaping into the air trying to look free, for example, it might still have worked, in a basic way. However, the value of addressing the target market in this more personal and more appealing way, is not just one of aesthetics (or even aerobics). The young girls who read this advertising will still be buying sanitary products when they're older. By showing understanding of the target market, the manufacturer can benefit from their trust later on.

For *The Economist*, the success of this apparently simple campaign is directly linked to what it knows of its readership. They are intelligent and want to be successful. The ads talk only to those points, never to any of the magazine's fascinating subject matter. Rather than boasting about *The Economist*'s writers, sales, articles, success in predicting events, it is content to identify with real accuracy the people it wants to talk to. This creates an intimacy with the product that is priceless in binding a consistent readership.

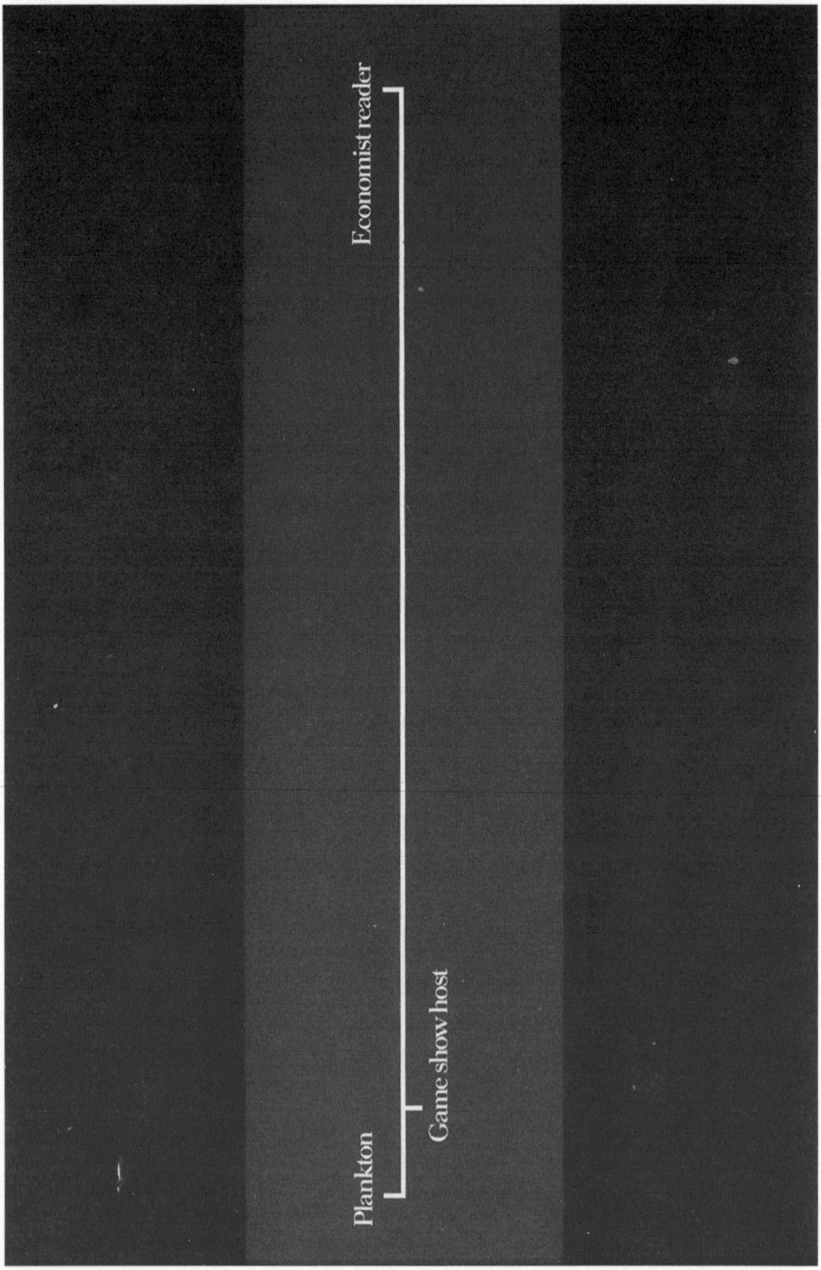
Economist reader
Game show host
Plankton

When you narrow down the market in this way, you don't have to shout so loud or so generally. You talk the same language as your audience and you're guaranteed a hearing.

It may seem odd to narrow your customer base when trying to make money. However, it makes sense if you're selling 300,000 units of a product and want to sell more, to talk intelligibly to the 3 million for whom the product is remotely appropriate, than vaguely to 60 million, including millions of children and retired people who don't need it.

If you think hard enough about your target market, award winners just spring into your head. The following ad was placed on top of a bus, to be read only by people who work in tall buildings. It couldn't have come from an understanding of the target market expressed only as 'Business Professionals, Social groups, A, B'. It had to have come from a seemingly banal observation that they tend to work in those big buildings in the middle of town.

The Lynx Effect

The Lynx brand of men's deodorant started life as one brand among many in Unilever's portfolio, marketed by its toiletries arm Elida Gibbs and advertised throughout the world by Lintas Worldwide. Lintas (a contraction of London International Advertising Services) was itself an offspring of the Unilever company, having started out as a department of the company.

The early Lynx advertising was glossy, but unsubtle. In one typical example, a cosmopolitan man arriving in a foreign port bumps into a sophisticated woman causing his wallet to fall to the ground. As she picks it up for him she takes the opportunity afforded to her to inhale his personal odour. She then hands back the wallet and makes it clear in no uncertain terms that she finds his smell alluring to the point of intoxication. Endline: Lynx. First impressions last.

Such advertising disports a certain attitude towards its market. As a pharmaceutical company, research is Unilever's strong suit, and it seems clear that this campaign is the product of the same sort of research as the tests they would run to establish the efficacy of a toothpaste or whether a shampoo has the unnecessary side effect of blinding a rabbit. In the case of Lynx this would mean that they gave the product to some of the proposed members of the target market, asked that they use it for a few weeks and that they fill in a form at the end of the process. The subjects would be asked to score their assessment of the product in terms of smell and effectiveness as well as state their personal position on the issue of body odour. The brief and the advertising followed in a regimented way straight from that data. The young men inhabiting the target market were sold to on the basis of the product's efficacy and the degree to which it solved their personal hygiene hang-ups.

And actually, it worked. Unilever saw a successful launch of the product in various countries. The product scored well and its solid performance meant that the same advertising model was used again and again. Every year or so the company commissioned a new execution, among whose mandatory ingredients were the man and woman in a hot country, the picking up of an item off the floor causing entry into personal space, followed by the female approval of the man's odour. The creative person's job was merely to select a country in which this drama would be performed.

Of course, in treating the target consumer like a laboratory guinea pig the conglomerate missed out on some salient details, the most loomingly obvious of which is the fact that they are not laboratory guinea pigs, but human beings. When the account moved to an advertising agency that operated outside of its own corporate structure they were able to see the world from another point of view. BBH, for it was they, has built its reputation on appealing to the youth market. The company HQ in London proudly suspends its black sheep symbol over Kingly Street, a precious relic from an early Levi's poster showing a black sheep facing the opposite way to a uniform crowd of white sheep, an image that is also, at the time of writing, the first to greet you on the BBH website.

Apart from assuming that the target market were only capable of Pavlovian responses, early Lynx marketeers burdened themselves with only examining their target consumer through the pinhole camera of his relationship with their product. It is perfectly obvious that the major motivator in a young male's life is not deodorization, but rather the benefits of deodorization. What Lynx could promise him was not the efficacy illuminated by the contrived situation of a girl sniffing him over like a dog looking for drugs. The promise was what happened once a girl falls into your lap. And so was born The Lynx Effect.

One early manifestation of this idea showed a young man accidentally falling into a prehistoric world inhabited only by young and beautiful women. Using a furry bikini top as a catapult to slay a two-headed monster he not only wins their immediate attention but also the bonus of inducing the whole tribe to remove their own bikini tops and wave them above their heads as weapons of war. Not politically correct even then, but the whole point of the term 'target market' is to acknowledge that other people do not necessarily think the way you do.

A more elegant 20-second commercial ran some years later, which showed a line up, at the start of a cycle sprint race in a velodrome. As is convention, four cyclists waited at the start line held round the waist by officials. At the siren, three make clean starts; the other cyclist, held by a female official, is hampered by the fact that she won't let go.

And the campaign reached its possible apogee with a recent episode in which we see a boy and girl rise from a crumpled bed and get dressed. In order to do so they take a tour round the streets of a city picking up items of clothing in reverse order to that in which they were discarded. The commercial ends in a supermarket as the two lovers put on their shoes next to two abandoned trolleys.

The distinction to be made between the First Impressions Last campaign and The Lynx Effect is that the first has a narrow understanding of who it is talking to. It is the product of a research methodology that smells consumers' armpits rather than sits them down with a beer and asks questions. It sees the target market from the scientist's point of view. The more rounded understanding of young unattached males portrayed by The Lynx Effect comes from seeing the world from their point of view. The result is that the campaign is far more resonant and endearing. Pleasant side effects for the advertiser include a smaller cost of production as they no longer need to throw money at foreign locations for a product whose true relevance resides on the street just outside their laboratory windows. Oh, and vastly greater sales.

Another side effect is that creative work sourced from the target market's world-view is almost always more enjoyable and less contrived in conception than that from the advertiser. It just makes more sense. There is less bafflement of the kind aroused by seeing a woman smell a man on a dockside. When thinking of the target market it's good to remember the nameless owner of the international hotel chain asked at a party given in his honour to give his personal message to the world. His message was, 'Please tuck the shower curtain into the bath', the point being that people can only see the world from their own point of view. Tautology, it may be, but there's nothing truer than a tautology.

The story of Lynx is not unusual. Many brands start out in the market with a clunky launch campaign, obsessed with itself as a product and its ingredients. The successful brands then refine their view of who they are talking to. It is a conversation played out in slow motion and at great expense, as both seller and buyer get to know each other. Those brands that do survive to refine their message often do so by having a good product or service message in the first place. Advertising, when it's targeted properly, can skip preliminaries involved in a conversation.

Rather than introduce yourself through half-effective advertising and await the response, why not pinpoint the target market from the off and have fully effective communication. In some instances, the long-term situation is not affected much either way, but there are others when it can mean the life or death of a brand, or even just life or death.

When HIV/AIDS first became a terrorizing disease, the public health message was conducted in Britain with a gravity and symbolism that seemed appropriate. But appropriate to whom? The media? Old ladies? Politicians?

The problem was that this was a real disease killing real people. The at-risk group were not being well served by millions spent making the right noises to opinion leaders and gossip columnists. The young and sexually promiscuous were not tuned in to paternalistic threats.

Around the time of this first public awareness campaign I took part in an exercise commissioned by the 'Right to Reply' programme for Channel 4. It researched the existing government campaign alongside alternatives. It was in this context that I contributed a campaign using Gray Jolliffe's character 'Wicked Willie' – essentially a talking penis. Needless to say it was a cartoon, and the campaign was explicit and irreverent. Just as needless to say, it worked far better in research groups. This research and its publicity had an impact where it mattered and the campaign's style was reflected in official AIDS awareness campaigns thereafter. Cartoon penises of various sizes and dispositions abounded on TV screens and doctors' notice boards throughout Europe and probably beyond for the simple reason that they worked. And with an issue like AIDS, it's really important for information to reach its target effectively.

Conclusion? When a campaign idea gets through as successfully as the BBH work for Lynx, you're almost certainly witnessing the 'target market effect'. And secondly, regardless of good taste, men will always pay attention to what their penises say.

RULE TWO:
DO RESEARCH

Far more thought and care go into the composition of any prominent ad in a newspaper or magazine than go into the writing of their features and editorials.
Marshall McLuhan, *Understanding Media*, 1964

One of the other ways to get to know your target market is to read the papers and magazines that they read, or to watch the programmes they watch. It's one of the more explicable coincidences in life that these also tend to be the media in which you're advertising to them.

MEDIA

Of course, when considering the media you have to be a little more selective in what you take out than when you are meeting the target market face-to-face. What you see and read, say, in a teen magazine tends to be very homogenous. The same is true of motoring magazines, computer magazines, lad's magazines, gardening magazines, *The Economist*, *The Sun*, *The Financial Times* and so on. In each publication almost everything in them, including the ads, seems to conform to a tribal identity.

It's important not to draw the wrong conclusion about how the medium should be used to your best advantage. Remember the magazine or paper itself needs to keep strictly to its house style in order to maintain its identity and reason for purchase. You (or your client) will be paying a healthy price to ride that identity in order to get into the sight line of the reader. It's a waste of that money if you overdo the conformity to the editorial style of communication. Instead, you should research the medium as an extension of the information-loading process started in Rule 1. In other words, having read the magazine, or the newspaper, or viewed the TV channel, this is not the moment to start writing ads. If we continue the metaphor of the tribe, you are not there to run around in the gang with everyone else, brandishing a spear and making similar noises. You are hoping to start a war cry that others adopt as their own. The term 'slogan' is indeed derived from an unspellable Gaelic word meaning 'war cry'. (The word's *sluaghghairm*, in fact.)

Background research into the technologically evolving media is something that needs to be ongoing, and is hardly unpleasant, as it merely involves watching movies, surfing the net and so on with a curious mind. If you know what can be done with visual effects, for example, it helps you to use them at their best. Slightly more difficult to acquire is insider knowledge of these media. It's useful to know, for example, a little about the costs of these processes.

MONEY

These days, if you can think it, you can show it. Unfortunately, there's no rule of thumb to say that if you can show it, your budget can afford it. There's not much worse than watching a spectacular effect done on the cheap. If you know you can't afford an idea, don't try to make it. If your idea is brilliant, but needs more money, fight for that money to be made available. Either way, don't kid yourself.

Don't be put off by tiny budgets. It may seem that lack of money is an excuse for not doing good ideas, because many impressive ads are very expensive. But in the end the ratio of cheap, good ads to expensive, good ads is fairly even. Note how many great press ads and posters consist of a few words and a logo. At the same time, if an idea is very funny or appealing it's more likely for people to give their services free or cheaply. A good idea often creates its own backers.

PRODUCTION METHODS

There's no limit to how much you can investigate about the various media you work in. Learn about photography, editing, lighting, film, computers, animation. Learn about production methods, film libraries, music search companies. Learn about the great names in advertising history; the copywriters, art directors, great agencies, designers, design movements. Learn about typography and illustration. Watch films and TV, theatre and cabaret, and make a mental note of useful actors, gags, ideas to remember for future use. Collect books that relate to the above areas, especially awards annuals for D&AD, and *The One Show*. Try unlikely-sounding art exhibitions, attend film festivals – in short, get out more.

Of course, you don't need all this from day one, but adopt the habit of hoovering up information all the time.

Look out for courses. Courses are enjoyable, social things to do in their own right, especially because the pressure is off. You don't need to remember the different filters for indoor and outdoor filming. A general knowledge is all you're after, something in the back of your brain that may one day inform your work.

In day-to-day work, you can probably convince yourself that you've satisfied Rule 1 very early in the process. For example, if you're writing a TV commercial aimed at middle-aged women, you could within seconds of the brief hitting your desk conclude, 'I know the target market personally, it's my mum, I spoke to her on the telephone last night.' As for researching the media, 'I watch television all the time so I've researched the medium too.' Simplistic as it sounds this actually isn't a bad way to think as it helps bring the idea of advertising down to earth. When Richard Philips wrote the Beatty commercials starring Maureen Lipman for British Telecom, he was instructed to think of the target market as his own mother and he did exactly that.

Likewise, if you are composing an important memo for your boss's eyes only, you may say to yourself, 'I know his or her foibles intimately and I receive memos all the time, and know which style works best.'

In both examples you could go further, putting a photo of your mother on the desk as a reminder when writing an ad, or phoning the boss's PA to see what kind of mood he or she is in. Both of these actions would help you carry out your task with little effort. A further increase in effort, say going to a research group of other people's mothers or taking the boss's PA to lunch to canvas a likely reaction to your views, would make a further contribution to the success of your end product. The principle is, the more effort you put in the better you will understand your task.

SUBJECT MATTER

Research more than you could possibly need on the subject you are to be working on. The reason is that if you research only according to your first impressions of a project, or according to preconceived ideas of what you will end up with, your end product will be restrained by the limits of your own conformity. Force yourself to research more broadly, even wastefully, as it will inform your writing and mystify your peers as to how you came up with such a novel piece of work. The internet is a fabulous tool for research, as you'll often find that your client already has a website. It's also good for picture research, ready-made links and obscure points of fact. Google everything. But be wary.

It can be a false friend. Sometimes its sheer speed and range can seem to give you an instant solution. So consider slower forms of research if there is time, like the library. This may sound like the sort of advice handed out in the 1940s to rookie copywriters wearing tweeds and smoking pipes. But try it once. You'll amaze yourself. Away from the office you'll find the subject becomes far more real to you: it's no longer something that's wandered into your office that needs to be wrestled out as quickly as possible. In a library, you realize grown men and women have spent years of their life considering it, or collecting data about it.

On the internet, information is arranged according to someone else's agenda and is better in certain areas than others. In the library, you can usually get a more rounded picture of your subject. Your own mind will become curious about some aspect of it.

A piece of copy written entirely in the office on the subject of ballpoint pens can take its raw material only from what's in your office at the time. Some notes from the manufacturer and a quick look at the product would probably lead you to start with something like, 'What's the best ballpoint pen you ever had?' As soon as it starts it already reads like a losing battle. You're obviously trying to find an interesting angle on ballpoint pens from inside your own head. Why should there be one there? What evolutionary benefit would it have? When people say 'Break the rules', what they often mean is, 'Come up with something fresh.' The internet would furnish you with a good number of places in the world to buy a ballpoint pen. But take a stroll down to a library, and you may end up with some real information. Your copy might now start, 'In 1834 a man fell into a drain in Budapest. An event which led to the invention of the ballpoint pen... .' Or, 'Mile for mile, the Smith & Jones ballpoint pen works out cheaper to run than a family saloon.' In reading them you feel that you are being served fresh ingredients. Here are two examples that make that point:

IF YOUR SKIN WAS THIS NEWSPAPER, THE SUN'S RAYS WOULD HAVE REACHED THE SPORTS PAGE.

Don't underestimate the power of the sun's UVA rays. Unlike UVB which burns, UVA passes right through the outer layers of your skin into the deeper living tissue.

The collagen (which gives the skin its elasticity) breaks down, eventually causing it to sag, wrinkle and age.

Help is at hand. Uvistat suncreams and lotions filter out a wider range of harmful UV rays than most other products on the market. The protection starts at Factor 6 and goes up to Factor 30 Ultrablock. (There's also an aftersun and lipscreen.) Naturally, we care for all skin types.

Uvistat is hypo-allergenic, lanolin free and non-greasy.

So the good news is you can let through some of the rays that help you tan and stop the ageing rays at page one.

If you'd like to know more, send the coupon to Uvistat, Windsor Healthcare Ltd, Bracknell, Berks. RG12 4YS.

Name

Address

Postcode

UVISTAT
THE GENTLE ART OF SUN CONTROL.

RULE THREE: ANSWER THE BRIEF

Unique Selling Proposition: getting a message into the heads of most people at the least possible cost.

Rosser Reeves, Ted Bates Agency

Having loaded your mind with information, you need to think seriously about producing some ideas. However, apart from making a note of any ideas that occur spontaneously, you should otherwise hold back. Remember Neil French's entreaty to 'avoid like genital warts the temptation to begin writing'. The reason for this is to ensure you're saying the right thing. No matter how much talent and technique is apparent in your advertising, at least 90 per cent of its effectiveness resides in the message you have decided (or been given) to communicate. So choose wisely and say the right thing.

The first rule here is set deeply in stone, yet is regularly transgressed. Say one thing and one thing only. This doesn't refer to the content of body copy or to any stylistic area, but to the underlying message. If your ad is designed to say a certain car model is safe, don't also say it's cheap. It's a hoary old chestnut but I might as well repeat the metaphor of the two balls, wherein it's impossible to catch two at once, if they're thrown to you in the street. Likewise, you can only catch one message at a time. (The actual number of balls varies according to the version of the metaphor you hear.)

The particular message to be conveyed is normally presented in the form of a brief. This might include the proposition or promise, along with a few words on tone of voice, target market, factual support and various kinds of guidelines and mandatory requirements. You can waste months of effort if you don't answer the brief. That's not to say that when good work is lost, it's because you've disregarded a signed piece of paper with the word 'Brief' at the top. You may well have answered your brief perfectly, and consequently feel justified in moaning when the work is unsuccessful. You may feel that forces were out of your control.

It's true, there is little more dispiriting than being told after months of work that the fruit of your efforts has merely illuminated where the brief was wrong in the first place. But it is part of your job to know that the brief is just a bit of paper, behind which is a product and a company's history, political problems, share price problems, competitive situation. This nebulous state of affairs is also part of your brief.

So, it's time to dig a little deeper.

PLANNING

Modern advertising agencies have planners and planning departments whose value is often questioned, most frequently by those in the creative department. The cause of this may be the fact that they do a similar job. Here, in simplified form, is how that happened.

It is accepted that there have been two significant structural changes on the creative side of advertising in the last 60 years. The first was when art directors were coupled with copywriters to work as teams. This happened at an agency called Grey Advertising in 1940s New York, when Phyllis Robinson and Bob Gage were put together as a 'copy-art' team by a far seeing Creative Director called Bill Bernbach. This meant that instead of a copywriter writing a headline, then handing it down to a visualizing department to create the final ad, they produced ideas together. This brought about a quantum leap in the quality of creative work, but in doing so created the need for the second epoch-making change, the introduction of planners.

Combining writer and art director into one executional unit ended the copywriter's pipe smoking, beard stroking days as he ruminated on the brand, the market, the client's psychological problems, and the wider brief in general. These ruminations may have created a dull, over-pedantic end product, but they were at least a link to the marketing process and a strategic rudder for the brand. With that gone, many clients found that brands were slipping around dangerously, with highly creative advertising being produced, demonstrably on-message, but mysteriously random in effect.

The trouble seemed to be that there was no longer someone in the advertising agency whose responsibility it was to say whether the message was the best one in the circumstances, and if not, what message should be in its place. It was during this era that David Ogilvy wrote *Confessions of an Advertising Man* (1963) and quoted Viscount Leverhulme's 'Half the money I spend on advertising is wasted, and the trouble is I don't know which half.' (This has been quoted in every book on advertising since then.)

The introduction of planners shortly afterwards re-centred this function into the advertising agency.

The roles of planner and copywriter overlap in that they both involve information gathering and deep thinking. Now that planners are fully fledged and departmentalized, creative teams aren't expected to do the deep thinking and it is accordingly hard for them to actively change the strategy. Alistair Crompton recounts the development of planners slightly differently in *The Craft of Copywriting*, saying that they grew out of account management. This is true, insofar as the actual personnel who became account planners were in general from the account rather than creative side. The vacuum they were filling, though, was created by this change of creative roles. Crompton also says, usefully, that 'a planner is the voice of the consumer inside the agency while the account managers represent the client, the client represents the product and the creative person, the campaign'. (It's not apropos, but a handy description of agency structure nevertheless.)

Planning is now a science and I suspect Viscount Leverhulme today would be able to quantify the value of every penny. There is a qualitative difference, however, between an individual's strategic thinking and that of a department. In Dave Buonaguidi's opinion, advertising has lost three generations of thinkers. So regardless of departmental considerations, it is always worth going through the strategic thinking yourself. It might take you somewhere different.

Start by answering the following questions:

- *What is the context?*
- *Given that context, what are you saying?*
- *Given what you are saying, what is the endline?*

This is a slight case of advertising by numbers. Obviously most brands come with an endline already in place. But even then it is important to consider the endline, if only to check it is still right and, if so, to anchor your conceptual work to it. In theory (and here's another rule for the masonic chisel) all ads should in some way prove their endlines.

The endline is a rudder throughout the creative process. Unfortunately, the best endlines are such effortless little phrases that even experienced advertising people often try to apply them as a cherry on a cake, after the work has been done. But nail the endline before you write the advertising, and decades of clarity can be yours.

In theory, then, an endline could be arrived at using the three steps mentioned.

Context

Be aware of the market information and circumstances that created the brief. Just as researching a little more about your target market can fling great ideas into your lap unbidden, so too can being truly aware about your client's situation. If you are an agency person it certainly makes selling your work a little easier. The fact that grand strategy is not part of your job description does give you at least one slight advantage over those for whom it is. You can think with objectivity about your client's predicament in a way that the chief executive may not. The chief executive may converse with other highly placed personnel in the marketplace but perhaps finds it difficult to assimilate the public's attitude from a bunch of figures in a survey. If you follow the rules thus far you will have this background information. You have the added benefit in that it is your job now to crystallize your findings into a piece of creative work to be delivered in a few weeks' time, before the situation moves on. In such a way, Andrew Rutherford, writer of 'Labour isn't working' (a 1979 Conservative Party poster discussed later) was able to crystallize the prevailing political situation, at just that moment in time when a poster was required.

To put it figuratively, you need to be something of a weather balloon. Raise your point of view above the day-to-day pressures, into the general forces that are acting on your client and your client's market.

What are you saying?

If your understanding of the context is correct, what you say follows fairly naturally. Take as an example Volvo, which started advertising in Britain with a range of cars that were perceived as safe, but boring. After careful thought they decided that what they had to do was make safety the absolute requirement for a car.

As time moves on and the market context changes, things become more difficult. In the 1980s the affluent people in their target market were no longer a cautious breed. They were having fun. The ads for safety were simple enough to be award winning, but BMW and VW were taking similar sterling qualities and expressing them as sexy engineering and quirky life enhancement respectively.

It was now imperative to make safety fun. This, as you can imagine, was not an easy task, and to begin with nothing much was accomplished. As there was a need to keep advertising new models and keep the name Volvo in the public eye, the agency did not have time to go through the whole thought process, and there were a number of unsuccessful commercials which seemed to dent the brand. One showed a car transforming magically into a white horse, which wasn't at all the sort of solid virtue one would expect of a Volvo. As the 1990s broke, the quality of the agency and the client prevailed as someone, somewhere wrestled the proposition into a logical one. Safety could be fun because it means you can do more dangerous things.

Despite the fact that Volvo don't use an endline, what they are saying as an advertiser is clear, logically connected to their context and therefore makes for some good advertising and for a brand that is in good shape.

Endlines

Having decided the all-motivating message, the next job is to seek the right expression. It may seem that searching for the perfect way of expressing your proposition is an overly poetic notion for a selling job. But this is the essence of advertising writing. It may be enough to say your proposition in a direct, no-nonsense fashion. 'We sell food cheaper' for example, would work if yours was a direct, no-nonsense company which really did sell food cheaper and had no other quality to recommend it.

Rarely can an endline be in a position to promise something that in itself is unique. Nevertheless it needs to say something. It must relate to its present context, yet last as something for salespeople in the field to pin their colours to for perhaps years to come. 'Something to put on the back of the lorry', as some people like to put it. Your endline therefore needs to carry what you want to say with the maximum possible distinction in the shortest possible number of words, not only to stand out from the rest, but also to stick in people's minds. Given so few words (usually) to play with, you need to try permutations of words, then analyse their subtle differences in meaning to find a word or phrase that clicks.

For example, saying 'More people prefer Smedley's' may mean the same as 'The majority of people prefer Smedley's', but there are subtle differences in connotation that are almost too small to define in a literary studies class. Yet, when used in a mass communication context, the latter's suggestion of recent scientific tests may be significant.

A real-life example is Tesco's 'Every little helps'. This clearly comes from a market imperative for cheapness, but avoids the connotation of low quality by using a colloquial phrase, rather than a direct claim along the lines of 'You can't buy cheaper'. This isn't a particularly remarkable achievement. Sainsbury's, their main rival, had already been running with 'Good food costs less at Sainsbury's' for many years. However, what 'Every little helps' does cleverly is address a prevailing media climate of suspicion, in which supermarkets are accused of profiteering, bad treatment of suppliers and general exploitation. The line places itself alongside the customer, as if the company was suffering the same problems as the harried housewife, struggling to lop the odd penny off the price of tomatoes. Ingenious.

Another good example that shows how helpful a line can be is Wallis's 'Dress to kill' from Bartle Bogle Hegarty, which is sound enough as an endline to set up some fashion press ads which are more enjoyable than usual.

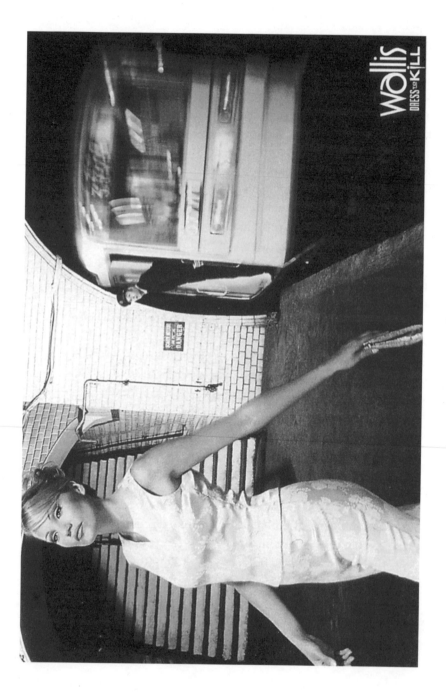

Endline Café

To truly appreciate the art of the endline it may be necessary to take a look at them as a genus, to go to a place where they can be found and observed in large numbers. No such habitat exists because endlines are not herd animals. They hunt alone.

The point of their existence is to define the world in terms of one product or service. It's Good to Talk cannot accept a world in which Say it With Flowers exists, and in a confined space they would fight to the death. So come with me to a notional space where they coexist in harmony.

The bad lines smoking and telling lousy jokes are at the back, ignored for the most part but tolerated because of the amount of money they waste trying to get noticed. It's an Equitable Life, Henry. It Just Feels Right, I've Got Mine, Setting the Standards. The establishment is happy to accept the wasted money they pour into the tills, but does so with a certain aloofness, knowing that they'll not come to much.

Relaxing in the comfy seats, the good lines are known to all and get freebies from the staff. These are the lines whose familiarity is born of good writing and of saying the right thing to the right people. But in many ways, the responsibility for the production and longevity of a good line is one instance in advertising where most of the credit should go to a client, whether it's a manager, marketeer, or proprietor, because they need to be spotted, often bought against conventional wisdom, sustained through the constant changes of personnel and market, and grown to the point that they guide the brand in perpetuity.

Say it With Flowers, Got Milk?, *Voorsprung Durch Technic,* Every Little Helps, Exceedingly Good Cakes, Reassuringly Expensive, The Future's Bright. The Future's Orange. If they spend a lot of time here it's because they never have to work very hard. Wherever they go they are recognized, make perfect sense and reinforce their own successes. They don't have to fight off challenges against competitors; those fights have been long won. In research their victories are relived and any replacement idea inspired by a new marketing manager or some tyro trying to make his mark is rapidly converted to so much folded polyboard in the research company's wheelie bin.

What do they talk about, these old timers? Old friends, presumably. What happened to Coke Is It? We don't see Pure Genius any more. Same with Eat More Fish, Slam in the Lamb, and Tea, Best Drink of the Day. Some pass without mourning. The absence of others causes disbelief. Nine Out of 10 Cats Prefer it? That can't be dead, can it? How about You Only Fit it Once So Fit the Best? Both still going, I think, perhaps so successful that they hardly need to be seen at all any more, except in direct mail or on product labels.

Perching on the arms of the sofas are the friends of the greats. They may not be endlines as such, but have such similar virtues that they belong in the same coterie. 'Hello Boys' is a headline from a Wonderbra poster run a long time ago with a £200,000 media spend, and still used in speech and by headline writers today. Soon it will have to leave, because it cannot do any more for the brand and has effectively become divorced from it. Another headline you might recall seeing is, 'You never own a Philip Patek watch, you just keep it for the next generation.' The constant rerunning of this immaculate thought with only a gradual evolution in the casting of its preppy Dad and son serves to reinforce its message with the perfect symmetry appropriate to a watch mechanism. It has never won an award, to my knowledge, and it has hardly become a playground chant. Nevertheless it feels at home with those campaign lines that have.

Lines that are the result of such good parenting have 360-degree virtue: they look good from any angle, whether it's customer, shareholder, worker, agency or supplier.

What distinguishes them? It's hard to say that they all have the same thing is common. In abstract terms, and with a slight shimmy into the territory of gurus and creationist pastors, what most seem to do is combine the authentic voice of their company, with an element of universal truth. *Voorsprung Durch Technic* seems to be the most obvious example of the authentic voice part of the equation – it's German. And while the actual sense of the company's motto, something about achieving a state of *Voorsprung* by means of *Technic* may escape the average car buyer, it is a universal truth that the Germanic approach to engineering is the one you want.

The Fourth Emergency Service is another helpful example. The AA is almost a public institution to us in the UK. We have three emergency services, and come to think of it automobile breakdown services are a kind of fourth. This also amply demonstrates the advantage that good endlines afford their creators and beneficiaries. The Fourth Emergency Service contains a universal truth alright, but only outside the walls of the RAC, who could easily have said the same thing at the same time and benefited from it in the same way. But now they can't. Ever.

Every Little Helps doesn't disturb the theory, being both authentic and true. Exceedingly Good Cakes is an authentically English sentiment appropriate to a brand called Mr Kipling. The universal truth? That the English make the best cakes? It's quite possibly true. Most of the universe, or at least that part that forms the brand's target market, will agree that Baclava and Florentines do not quite nail the concept of cake. Checkers, a burger chain in the United States, says something very, very true in its endline 'You gotta Eat!', yet still has an authentic and charming corporate tone of voice.

The proposition can also be proved in the negative. Tennants lager ran with a line, 'I've got mine' for several years, which if referring to a pint of Tennants surely isn't true for most people most of the time. Nor has it a plausible tone of voice for the brewer. And one could go on. Tea is rarely the best drink of the day. Eat More Fish has a nice feel about it, but the voice seems to come from nowhere. And Slam in the Lamb is the same thing, except that it rhymes. In the end, it matters not whether the theory is correct, and entry to the pantheon or the Endline Café is meaningless fiction. But if you are in that rare circumstance, where you are entrusted to devise a powerful endline for someone or something, it may be worth using the concepts of universal truths and authentic voices to start the process.

Planning conclusion

It may be that some briefs really don't require this planning stage. Obviously this applies to certain price announcements and 'sale now on' messages. But even then, making sure that you're aware of the back-story is really just another aspect of doing your research. Its importance also varies according to the nature of the product. If you're advertising a cooking pot that is more hard wearing than another, go to it. The manufacturer's background may be worth investigating, but the best end result is likely to be a simple demonstration of this proposition.

The idea that during your career you're going to be briefed to produce many great demonstrations of cooking pots seems rather quaint. Nowadays the companies with money to spend seem to be media conglomerates, international brands, computer companies, software houses, banks and other firms whose products can't exactly be smashed against a wall to show their craftsmanship. Often the point of difference for such institutions is not to be found in their product or service, but in their character, or in something as intangible as their attitude.

To work on such subjects, the nebulous brief behind the brief is all-important. What at first sight may seem like a straightforward piece of publicity may in reality be a reaction to the threat of merger, or a simple way of spending £200,000 before the end of the financial year, in which case they may be prepared to produce something challenging and different. It is surprising how often apparently straightforward advertising briefs have turned out to be aimed at least partially at a company's own employees. When Philips launched its 'Let's make things better' endline worldwide, it had one meaning for the consumer in the high street and another for the staff of that company, who had just endured a global rationalization programme. A classic *sluaghghairm* for the Philips tribe.

Finally, an endline needn't just be a collection of mildly invigorating words at the bottom of a page, tucked beneath the logo. It can also be the idea of the advertising itself. The AA was one motoring organization among many scrabbling after memberships outside supermarkets, until someone, somewhere, elevated it to the 'fourth emergency service'. The ads themselves have never been memorable, but the idea rings out in the endline and has had a real and damaging effect on its competitors.

French Connection did a similar thing with their FCUK campaign. FCUK is hardly even a line but as the encapsulation of nonconformity, it had an extremely happy effect on the company's profits.

Both examples show how thinking about the right endline also leads you to consider tone of voice.

TONE OF VOICE

Part of answering a brief is finding the exact tone of voice. Although this is only a subsection in a book of copywriting rules, it could also be a book in its own right.

A study has shown that the meaning people extract from each other during conversation is 7% down to the words we hear and 38% based on the tone those words are said in (the remaining 55% is based on body language).

Alan Young, St Lukes

The reason this subject is so much bigger than simply communicating product values to a customer is that it also impacts on the

Do we drive our mechanics too hard?

For most people, going under a car is the end of their career.

For a Volkswagen mechanic, it's just the beginning.

He starts with the humble spark plug.

And works his way up to the digilent electronic system.

He takes every part apart. And puts it back together again.

Over and over and over again.

Until he can show us where every bolt, every washer and every nut goes.

What every part does.

And how to service every single one of them.

Then we really turn the screws on him.

Because, when he's not working on a Volkswagen, Volkswagen are working on him.

At one of our training schools.

There he spends seven hours a day studying the mechanics of the car.

So, by the end of his apprenticeship, he knows his Volkswagen bumper to bumper and sill to sill.

All this is part of the quaint Volkswagen notion that the service has to be as good as the car itself.

It's the kind of madness that makes us make our cars the way we do.

The sanest things on wheels.

identity of the company itself. In organizations where the corporate or brand tone of voice is clearly understood, it's a positive force for a company because it helps all its workers 'live the brand' as one marketing manager puts it. The benefit is a clear and intuitive understanding by all staff of the goals and approach of their organization.

Wolff Olins echo this thought in their *Guide to Corporate Identity*, published by the Design Council:

The fundamental idea behind a corporate identity programme is that in everything the company does, everything it owns and everything it produces, the company should project a clear idea of what it is and what its aims are.

A company's advertising falls into all three of Wolff Olins' categories. It is the very expression of what a company does and owns and is itself a company product. The consultancies who advise on corporate identity tend to have a design background and interpret briefs visually. However, there is often a great benefit in considering how your company's identity may be represented in the sort of language used and the kind of ideas expressed.

Tone of voice seems very important, for some reason, in car advertising. We can all identify the VW tone of voice after years of consistency.

Audi too seems to have found its voice and the TV advertising forgets the car completely and talks only about the man. (It is a car for the male driver only, apparently.) One of the best examples of pure tone of voice is the long-running *Economist* campaign. They manage to do everything from billboards down to special offer inserts with exactly the same simple, superior tone, no matter what the subject. In turn, part of what defines and refines a tone of voice is consistency.

Virgin in all its manifestations maintains a wilful, youthful, counter-cultural tone of voice throughout everything it says and does, whether it's taking on British Airways in court or launching a phone tariff.

65

Innocent Smoothies exist in a space all of their own making, with a cunningly innocent tone of voice, immediately recognizable, and the tone on its packaging is identical to the tone on TV.

The closer Audi gets to pure steely Germanic inscrutability in its tone of voice the less it actually has to say.

What these very different brands all have in common is that almost everything we think of them spontaneously comes from their tone of voice. Eternally useful as a great endline is, a great corporate voice has the potential to be in some ways even more powerful. Virgin can start a company in any sector it likes, because everybody will immediately recognize its role in that sector through its tone of voice. Virgin Cheese then, would be the rock and roll version of the leading brand that breaks new ground in ways that benefit the consumer. (Hard to imagine, I know.)

Just as having 'a voice' rather than a line gives you flexibility to enter different markets with a ready-made identity, so it also allows you to express yourself through different media, and run widely different campaigns without worrying about fragmenting what you stand for.

Virgin Mobile ran a campaign using the line, 'The devil makes work for idle thumbs'. The line for a start is clearly liberated from the usual hankerings of chairmen and advertising purists in that it doesn't aspire to last for ever. It's freed from the role of containing the brand statement, from having to say, 'Phones that make you appear cool'. It can spiral off into another world where advertising isn't selling; it's a source of fascination it itself.

The tone of voice is what ties the ads back to the main brand. It seems not to matter what it's saying, but who it's saying it to, and how it's speaking. But of course, it does matter what it's saying:

We are using online viral and buzz marketing as a strategic part of our 'idle thumbs' marketing campaign in order to broaden awareness

*of our new 3p text tariff – particularly among the culture-driving,
technology-savvy online viral community.*

James Kydd, brand director for Virgin Mobile

What appears to be an inconsequential game to the target market is in fact simply a logical way to get through to that market. The rich experience of the campaign is a cultural one, made possible by not enslaving itself to a conventional advertiser's approach. The corporate voice is a marketing property that has special skills to get through boundaries, round walls, under radar, where a traditional approach would give itself away at the first checkpoint.

It is tempting to overstate the financial value of owning a unique tone of voice but the case study of Virgin Mobile is a startling one. As I've described already, on entering any market Virgin had a ready-made, well liked tone of voice as the people's champion, on a mission to simplify and make more enjoyable the experience of using the product or service. Mobile phones were ripe for simplification. A university study calculated that at the time of Virgin's entry there were a million different possible tariffs on offer between the big four players in the market. Not much fun. Virgin's first campaign was aimed at communicating their inherently simple offering of one rate for all. The Virgin Mobile brand took off exponentially and it built up an impressive customer base – the measure of success in the mobile phones market. The value of being able to do this from scratch is enormous, but factor in the small detail that Virgin did not actually own any of the stuff you make phone networks from and it's even more impressive. No networks, no shops, no masts, no bandwidth. They were a virtual network, simply buying the capacity they needed for their customers from another of the players in the market. Virgin's corporate voice meant they could start a £300 million brand from nothing, with nothing. Could yours do that?

Before you throw this page down on your Chairman's desk and say, 'Hey boss, we got to get ourselves into this tone of voice business', there are two caveats.

The first is that your tone of voice does carry with it certain limitations. Virgin Mobile is a success story, but partly this is down to the fact that they recognized early on that though they entered with the intention of appealing to all users, their tone of voice skewed their appeal to the youth. As it happened that was just the very thing to be doing. The youth were the key group for mobile phones as they had a burning interest in the new uses for the phones and their opportunities for self-expression, and Virgin's appearance was very welcome. The existing big four mobile networks, to quote one member of one research group, 'weren't interested in me if I weren't a businessman'.

In the light of Virgin's success this is clearly the more minor of the two caveats. The second is that while an Audi, Virgin, Pret a Manger or Gap tone of voice may seem to the consumer like an effortless exhalation, it isn't quite so easy. Far from being the last coat of paint applied to an ordinary company, what characterizes all these companies is that the tone of voice goes all the way through every part of the company, and not just communications.

In fact, every company has a tone of voice, whether it advertises or not. This is self-evidently true if you think of a company you may have phoned recently. The image you have of this company will be made up of the publicity you have seen for the company and the mood and tone of the person you happened to speak to that day, and the percentage of that impression created by the call-handler is probably greater than the millions they spent on advertising and reaching you by mail shot.

In fact everything contributes to tone of voice. How you publicize your prices, the staff in the showrooms, your non-smoking policy, your stationery, your speed of replying to e-mails, your company cars, reps' hairstyles, your MD's quotes in the local paper, your coffee machines, your invoices, the way you treat suppliers, your lifts. They all communicate. Virgin know this. Gap know this. Innocent and Audi know this. Their cultures will pervade every part of the experience of visiting a Virgin, Gap, Innocent or Audi premises.

A difference to be aware of is that between a trained voice and an untrained one. The untrained voice is typically raw and immediate and sometimes devastatingly successful. The in-house advertising departments of easyJet, Gap and Benetton all have, or had at some point, colossal cut-through. But Bernard Mathews always strikes me as the quintessential untrained marketing voice. You rarely see him these days on the small screen, but the fortune that presumably keeps him away was built up from some highly derided commercials some decades ago, in which he bragged of his turkeys' firm white meat with no professional help whatsoever. It's hard now to buy his Turkey Twizzlers without still hearing his gumbooted vowels in the distance, even though the nearest they've been to well fed white meat is an occasional visit from the extrusion machine repairman.

The point is that just as a trained, youth-focused, rock 'n' roll tone of voice was trusted by young purchasers of mobile phones, a simple untrained farmer's tone of voice was trusted by mums for meat products. The reason tone of voice can be so powerful is that it is the final leap of contraction. Once you've reduced a brand's offering to a few words, a proposition, mantra, *sluaghghairm,* endline or whatever it might be, to reduce it one step more, to a voice or an attitude, is to become real and trusted to the target market, with all the pleasant, long-term consequences that implies.

CAMPAIGNS

For the copywriters, the planning stage can be shortened if one is experienced or blessed with intuition. But there is an advantage in going the long way round, discussing the bigger picture fully and deciding on or reconciling yourself to where a brand is going and where it needs to go. Airing this, particularly with the client for whom you are working, enables you then to produce advertising on a theme that will stay relevant in years ahead. You have, in other words, a campaign. This is a Holy Grail of advertisers. It makes you big, in the way that *The Economist* is and *Business Week* is not. It opens an exclusive channel of communication between you and your audience. Whatever you say, you have an immediate platform from which to say it. The great campaigns thunder on from generation to generation and elevate their subjects in ways their competitors can only wonder at.

A great advertising campaign imparts a special quality, an intangible but important extra value to the product being advertised. The ads become more effective than sales tools, they become an extension of the product itself.
Larry Dobrow, When Advertising Tried Harder

This is where advertising and propaganda part ways. With a campaign, in which each execution sets out to demonstrate the campaign line, it is essentially saying that the proposition or promise is so true that it can be demonstrated again and again. Each individual execution adds to the stockpile of proof and deepens the relationship with the viewer. Some large advertisers do however use the techniques of propaganda, where a single execution or phrase is repeated so often that it becomes accepted as orthodoxy. Certain advertisements have been repeated almost in exactly the same form for decades. I'm thinking here of those for soap powders, medicines, cosmetics and shampoo brands of the sort owned by giant multinational companies. Being accepted as orthodoxy, or brainwashing as it could be known, is expensive, as the message really does have to be pretty constant. To be fair, such companies depend on steady and predictable growth rather than short bursts of brilliant success interspersed with possible failure. They have excellent products, vast research departments and global operations employing thousands of people. They don't like unpredictability and are prepared to pay the price. For propaganda to work you have to simply outgun conflicting worldviews, and as the media environment becomes more unwieldy even the biggest of the multinationals have been found doing more interesting work.

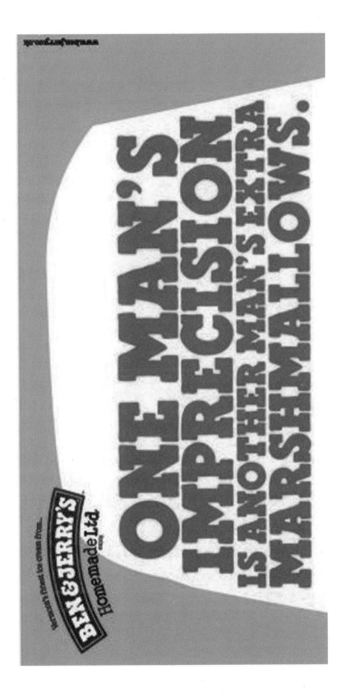

RULE FOUR:
BE RELEVANT

Readability is credibility.

Attributed to Philip Larkin

You are now in a position to write ads. You know the background, you know who you are talking to, you have information from the brief about the current imperatives and the direction you are travelling. You need nothing more. If you produce ideas using research into these areas you are certain your ideas will be relevant. Other areas might strike you as interesting, or fashionable, but whatever you write has to be there for a reason.

Don't put things in on a personal whim, for example, because you find it funny or you saw it on TV last night. Nor should you try to steer your copy round so that you can fit in a particular joke or clever form of words. Nor should you put things in to fill up space or time. If you feel you are, either change the length requirement, or change the idea to one suitable to the time or space you're working to.

Likewise, if you're working in print and you feel you're rambling on, donate the space to the picture. Or even to the surrounding white space. This is where the expression 'Less is more' actually means something. The more you leave out the more important the remainder appears and the more powerful it looks on the page.

Some things that seem obviously relevant should still be left out because they're redundant. Avoid saying the same thing in words as you're saying in pictures. If you're saying 'This dog collects sticks' and showing a dog, there's some redundancy. Show a dog and say, 'Wilberforce is a collector of sticks', and there's something going on between the words and the picture that's more involving.

Check the ticket of every fact you include. Does it have the right to be there? Is it there just because that's the way it's always done? Is it an important part of the product? Even if it is, is it an important part of the reason to buy the product?

However, with all this avoiding and getting rid of, you could end up with nothing at all. If you get rid of everything that's not relevant to your target market and are left with nothing, that should tell you something very important about your brief. However, to be more positive, how do you find what is relevant? Often it's right in front of you, looking absolutely boring and unusable.

Take an example from the burgeoning industry of TV trailer writing. There are so many channels nowadays that there are more programmes to trail and, given the increasing competition, more reason to trail them. It may seem a straitjacket to use clips from the programme or film itself, and not very original either. But it's hard to embody proof in the trailer if you stray into a more creative area (though not impossible). You may want to show the audience, saying what they like about the programme, or a psychologist analysing it. So long as it's relevant, it can work.

METAPHOR

Advertising by metaphor often appeals to creative people (or to people trying to look creative) as it seems to make the subject or product appear important and deep. The trouble is it can also look self-conscious. What's worse, it can also imply that the client is not prepared to speak directly.

When you consider the creative alternatives, it may seem that to bed your idea in reality is boring. However, you don't gain much by using clever comparisons. The clever comparisons that do work often turn out on further examination to be not so fanciful after all.

One example is the ad for a four-wheel drive Landrover, which showed a baby walking towards a ramp. As it reached the ramp it instinctively dropped on to all fours to continue. This appears to be a comparison, but in fact it's a dramatization of basic physics. Likewise, a seat belt campaign showed an elephant coming through from the back seat of a car during an impact. This would have been a poorer idea were it not for the fact that the elephant wasn't a memory aid, but a true representation of the actual tonnage of force involved when unrestrained back seat passengers jerk forward in a crash. But you don't even need an elephant.

Take these two D&AD silver winners from donkeys years ago, Volvo and Nike. The former shows a man speaking to camera about safety features while his car is crashing, the second shows, basically, people kicking footballs on a football pitch, wearing Nike football boots.

The writers haven't strayed an inch from their subject matter. However, by not being tempted into madcap creative solutions they have clearly understood what it is that involves their target market in the subject. Volvo drivers really are interested in the little features of their vehicle, and would probably love to be talking about them during a crisis. As for people who play football, it's almost too obvious to mention that they love watching football too. Both of these commercials prove the benefit of not ignoring the obvious.

Relevance is, however, a two-way street. Just as intriguing the consumer is pointless if you're not relevantly

involving the product, so the product is not well served if the ad you produce doesn't touch the lives of the intended purchaser.

Tony Cullingham, head of the copywriting course at West Herts College, occasionally tells a student he'll write 2000 words of copy and guarantees the student will read every word. The next day he hands over 2000 words of copy describing the student in as much detail as a little research allows. Naturally, every word is read. Your research into the target market should allow you to replicate this experiment, with the slight added complication of introducing the product.

Essentially the rule 'Be relevant' concerns communication. This needs to be said because you can follow all the rules perfectly, you can actually produce fabulous poetry on behalf of your client, but it won't be good copy. Communication is a very special concept because it combines the idea of a message sent with a message received.

To make the point, draw a blob on a piece of paper. The blob is you. You have a history, a background, a state of mind, a set of ambitions. It's also your company, with its history, background, present situation and set of goals. It's also your client and their history, background, problems and goals. The blob now contains your entire professional universe. And it's very small.

Now draw another blob on the same piece of paper, to represent the person you're talking to. He or she is not interested in your career, or the company you speak for. You could put everything together logically and perfectly and he or she would ignore it. Why? Because he or she also has a history, a background, a state of mind and a set of goals and ambitions, enough to fill up his or her life without any input from you. You, your company and, believe it or not, your client could disappear forever and this person wouldn't care. If they did care, why would we be asked to promote them? The National Health Service doesn't employ copywriters and art directors to persuade people to come in to have their lives saved. It doesn't need to.

THERE IS A SPELLING MISTAKE IN THIS ADVERTISEMENT.
THE FIRST PERSON TO SPOT IT WILL RECIEVE $500.

No, it's not in this line.

Or, you'll have guessed, in this line, either.

You're going to have to read this entire page, with the eyes of a school examiner, to spot it.

Which, when you think, makes it rather a good advertisement, doesn't it? Since ads, like the editorial they sidle up to, are written to be read.

How many of the other ads in this week's 'Media' are going to get this amount of attention?

One, maybe? Two?

It's more than likely that you haven't read *any* of them. Be honest, now:

You've given them the same treatment you give those suspiciously friendly encyclopaedia salesmen, who knock on your door and ask for five minutes of your time.

No, thank you: Slam the door. (Or in this case, turn the page.)

No sale. And we don't blame you. You saw the sell coming. Why waste your time?

The majority of ads are like that, too. Predictable, dull, and not very well presented.

They resolutely ignore the fact that the average consumer sees one thousand, six hundred advertising messages every day, and would be perfectly content not to see any at all.

You see, with the possible exception of seven year old brats with a passion for Teenage Mutant Ninja Turtles, PEOPLE DON'T LIKE ADS. There, we've said it. In a publication dedicated to the creed that advertising is a profession comparable only in its saintliness and altruism with being one of Mother Teresa's little helpers, we've spilt the beans:

We are not universally popular: If spacemen came down and took every person connected with advertising away for dissection, it would be a long time before we were missed. And even then, it would be because people discovered that their newspapers had become more interesting, and their TV programmes more enjoyable, for our absence.

(See? Heresy spoken out loud. And still we write. No thunderbolts from on high. God doesn't like ads, either.)

And yet...

And yet, in the face of reams of irrefutable evidence to the contrary, the majority of advertising agencies (and let's spread the blame a bit, their clients, too), persist in the belief that this just ain't so.

They sincerely believe that buying a space also guarantees readership of whatever they fill it with.

Sadder still, the higher the cost of the space, the more tense and creatively constipated they become, and the more safe and generic is their message: It's a new rule; the bigger the budget, the blander the ads.

Even the relatively enlightened feel that if they find, and mention, some semblance of a benefit in that space, they've *really* done a good job.

That by some miracle, the consumer is going to home in on their ad, shrieking "Just what I've always wanted!"

Sure. If your benefit is "Free Beer".

OK; *definitely*, if your benefit is "Free Beer". But if it's not, you're in big trouble.

You're going to be thrown in there with washing powders that get clothes whiter, toothpastes that taste nicer, tires that grip better ...

In other words, you're going to be ignored.

Don't misunderstand us, please. If your product has a substantial benefit over its competitors, you'd be mad not to tell everyone. The point is, it'd be mad to think that's *all* you had to do.

The public, as we've said, has become immune to everyday advertising.

For an ad to succeed these days, it has to work on many levels. It has to be relevant to the reader: It has to speak to him in language he can relate to: If there *is* a benefit to crow about, it has to be a benefit that's important to the *consumer*, not just to the manufacturer: To revert to the door-to-door salesman analogy, it has to look good ...the sort of person you'd invite into your home; the sort of advertisement you'd welcome into your mind...

But most of all, it has to be 'different'.

It has to jump from the page, or leap off the screen, screaming "Read me! Watch me!"

And it has to do so with a degree of seduction in its voice, rather than the foot-in-the-door brazen insistence, that leads only to the zap, the flip, and the broken toe.

Now. Doubtless there are sceptics out there who may say that this particular advertisement meets none of the criteria that it has been at such pains to expound.

That it is visually dull, dull, dull.

That it's criminally overwritten: That it's also a stupid concept, and that the one and only reason that they're reading it is to find the spelling mistake and qualify for $500 in the currency of their choice.

They may, of course, be right. (Found it yet, by the way? Keep going; concentrate.)

But at the Ball Partnership we'll do anything to get people to read ads.

Ours. Or yours.

They'll save your life for free and consequently their waiting rooms are always full. What the NHS does do is advertise for nurses to work long hours and get very little financial reward. Now that's something that needs good advertising, and gets it.

The very fact that you get a brief at all should tell you that just at the moment, the people you're talking to don't care (or don't care enough) about what you do. In a situation where people don't care, you need to find a point of contact. The nursing ads do that by appealing to our desire to help others. Suddenly, far from being the worst looking job on the table, the satisfaction it offers is unique. In terms of the two blobs on your page, it draws an X on the page between them. It creates something that's visible and meaningful for both parties.

As the writer of many of Apple's greatest ads, Steve Hayden, puts it, 'Search for some way to relate the tiny, constricted world the clients live in to the larger sunnier world people actually care about.' This is what you are looking for. In the words of *Zen in the Art of Archery*, you must think from the point of view of the archer and target at the same moment. Or to put it less profoundly, you need an advertising idea.

There is one thing stronger than all the armies in the world, and that is an idea whose time has come.

Anon

Ideas are essentially problem solving. If a cat's stuck in a tree you might solve the problem by having a bright idea, such as attaching a basket to a pole, which you then put into action. The cat has to figure out what your game is and decide whether it wants to play along. An advertising idea is the opposite of that: it's a means by which you put ideas into the heads of others. For example, in this case, by putting a fish in the basket.

To put that wisdom in slightly more vocational fashion, imagine it as an advertising brief, with the proposition, 'Cat's like fresh fish'. To convey this proposition without an advertising idea

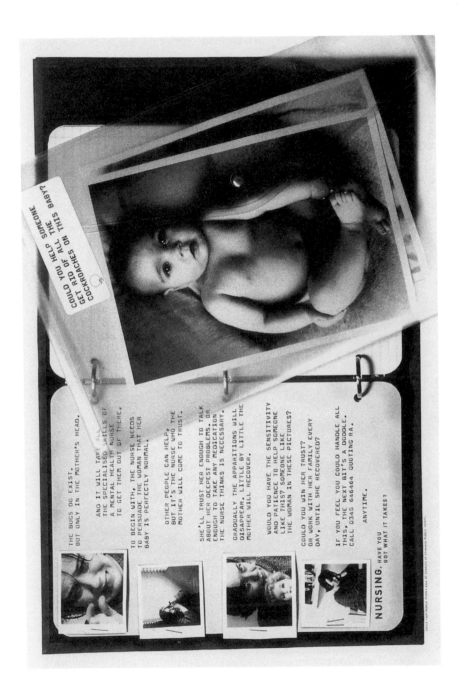

COULD YOU HELP SOMEONE GET RID OF ALL THE COCKROACHES ON THIS BABY?

THE BUGS DO EXIST, BUT ONLY IN THE MOTHER'S HEAD.

AND IT WILL TAKE ALL THE SPECIALISED SKILLS OF A MENTAL HEALTH NURSE TO GET THEM OUT OF THERE.

TO BEGIN WITH, THE NURSE NEEDS TO PERSUADE THE WOMAN THAT HER BABY IS PERFECTLY NORMAL.

OTHER PEOPLE CAN HELP, BUT IT'S THE NURSE WHO THE MOTHER WILL COME TO TRUST.

SHE'LL TRUST HER ENOUGH TO TALK ABOUT HER DEEPEST PROBLEMS. OR ENOUGH TO TAKE ANY MEDICATION THE NURSE THINKS IS NECESSARY.

GRADUALLY THE APPARITIONS WILL DISAPPEAR, LITTLE BY LITTLE THE MOTHER WILL RECOVER.

WOULD YOU HAVE THE SENSITIVITY AND PATIENCE TO HELP SOMEONE LIKE THIS? SOMEONE LIKE THE WOMAN IN THESE PICTURES?

COULD YOU WIN HER TRUST? OR WORK WITH HER FAMILY EVERY DAY, UNTIL SHE RECOVERED?

IF YOU FEEL YOU COULD HANDLE ALL THIS, THE NEXT BIT'S A DODDLE. CALL 0345 646464 QUOTING RA.

ANYTIME.

NURSING. HAVE YOU GOT WHAT IT TAKES?

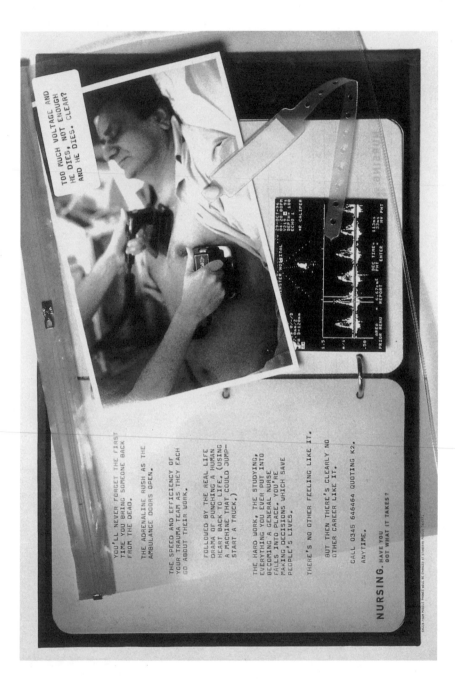

TOO MUCH VOLTAGE AND
HE DIES, NOT ENOUGH
AND HE DIES. CLEAR?

YOU'LL NEVER FORGET THE FIRST
TIME YOU BRING SOMEONE BACK
FROM THE DEAD.

THE ADRENALINE RUSH AS THE
AMBULANCE DOORS OPEN.

THE SPEED AND EFFICIENCY OF
YOUR TRAUMA TEAM AS THEY EACH
GO ABOUT THEIR WORK.

FOLLOWED BY THE REAL LIFE
DRAMA OF PUNCHING A HUMAN
HEART BACK TO LIFE. (USING
A MACHINE THAT COULD JUMP-
START A TRUCK.)

THE HARD WORK, THE STUDYING,
EVERYTHING YOU EVER PUT INTO
BECOMING A GENERAL NURSE
FALLS INTO PLACE. YOU'RE
MAKING DECISIONS WHICH SAVE
PEOPLE'S LIVES.

THERE'S NO OTHER FEELING LIKE IT.

BUT THEN THERE'S CLEARLY NO
OTHER CAREER LIKE IT.

CALL 0345 646464 QUOTING K2.
ANYTIME.

NURSING. HAVE YOU
GOT WHAT IT TAKES?

you might show a picture of a cat eating a fresh fish photographed in a pleasant glow with the line, 'Cat's like fresh fish'. The person walking past such a poster will not deduce anything from it, but will perhaps add the image to his or her memory bank as an experience. If, instead, the poster showed (as one did some time ago) a cat in a welder's mask using an oxyacetylene torch to break into the fridge, the same line works differently. The proposition is effortlessly transported from the advertising brief into the customer's brain.

This distinction is found in an excellent advertising book, *When Advertising Tried Harder*, written to commemorate the work of Bill Bernbach and his agency. You hardly need to read it as the title makes the point about good and bad advertising very clear. Unless your ad contains an advertising idea, it's not trying hard enough. You're merely adding to the customer's experience of a hectic world. If your ad does contain an advertising idea, you are creating thoughts in the minds of consumers that weren't present before. What is beautiful is that the human brain actually enjoys solving problems. Good advertising doesn't have to pollute the world.

RULE FIVE: BE OBJECTIVE

Like the advertising people, I don't ask you to trust me without offering a respectable reference.

Lady Tippius, in *Our Mutual Friend*

This is one area where the practice of advertising for the creative or the marketing professional is counter-intuitive. If a person were to be dragged off the street and instructed to produce a poster or TV commercial, the likelihood is that they would interpret this to mean to speak subjectively. They would express the product's benefit in a way that was basically an opinion. It tastes great, or is the best on the market. Partly, the lay person does this because most of the advertising they see appears to do this. And the reason why 90 per cent of advertising does this is willingness to please. This is not to impugn the practitioners themselves, exactly, but more the structure of their employment. Luckily, this subject can be reasonably adjudged to fall outside the eight rules of copywriting, so I won't pursue it beyond saying that when a company pays an agency or an individual to advertise a product, there is an understandable human urge for the payee to compliment the payer. Having agreed a large fee, it's natural for the recipient to feel like producing work that gushes about the product and, by implication, the wisdom and natural acumen of the client.

Obviously I'm not recommending marching into a managing director's office with a poster stating that his or her product is fourth best in the market and slightly overpriced. Or am I?

Stella Artois today is one of the biggest brands in the British brewing trade. Twenty years ago it certainly wasn't. It was a relatively small name in the market, partly because it was a premium beer with a premium price. Some mug, admittedly working for a good agency with a good relationship with its client, blundered into a managing director's office with an endline, 'Reassuringly expensive'. In the interim it has plugged away with this strategy that recognized the product as over-priced. Indeed, they still do, even though it no longer appears any more expensive than comparable beers. Obviously, the line puts an important spin on the quality of expensiveness by using the word 'reassuringly'. Nevertheless, the fact that the sentiment seems to have come from an objective source by admitting the product is expensive, makes a convincing implication that there is a legitimate reason for that high price in the buyer's mind. Namely, the beer tastes better than the average.

The classic example of this truth-telling strategy is that of Avis, the car rental company, which took its position in the US market in the 1960s (number two behind Hertz) as a convincing argument to choose their service. Their endline was, 'We try harder'.

The modern word for this is 'spin'. But this rule is not about the art of spin. Once you have chosen to admit that your beer is more expensive, it doesn't take a genius to prefer 'reassur-ingly' to 'pointlessly' as a qualifier. The rule is to find an objective fact that you can use as a reason to buy. The nearer you stay to relevant facts the less your words sound like puffery.

The 'Need I say more' approach is very persuasive and the best way of achieving it is with an unarguable demonstration. One of the most famous examples of demonstration advertising is the poster for Araldyte adhesive. A real car is stuck on to a poster with the line, 'It also sticks handles to teapots.'

Another example is an ad I remember for a see-through glass saucepan. The glass pan was put on a stove as the voiceover asks if such a pan could be as heat resistant as a normal metal saucepan. A metal saucepan is placed inside the glass one, and the metal one melts in front of our eyes.

Facts speaking for themselves are very convincing. You can't always stick cars to posters, but you can embody proof in everything that you write. An example of this is Doyle Dane Bernbach's snowplough commercial for Volkswagen. We open on a VW Beetle driving through thick snow in the early dawn. It arrives at a shed. Meanwhile, a male voiceover says, 'Have you ever wondered how the man who drives the snowplough gets to the snowplough?' We then see a man's feet get out of the car and trudge to a larger vehicle. The voiceover continues, 'This one drives a Volkswagen. So you can stop wondering.' It's a beautifully simple advertising idea that exudes self-evident proof of the reliability of the car, even though on closer examination there is no actual proof there.

In the spirit of 'Need I say more', I shall indeed say no more and leave it to the examples to prove the point of how convincing objective proof can be.

HOW TO IMPROVE A GOLF'S TURNING CIRCLE.

"I can't drive a great big car like a Volvo estate around town," we hear you say.

Actually, you can. The Volvo 940's power steering, excellent all round visibility, and surprisingly light clutch make battling with city traffic a pleasure. Well, almost a pleasure.

And when it comes to tight corners (and tight parking spaces) the Volvo has been specially designed to out-manoeuvre much smaller cars.

In fact at 32.5 feet, its turning circle is tighter than a Volkswagen Golf's.

Then there's Volvo's familiar front and rear crumple zones, the steel bars reinforcing its doors, and, of course, its rigid steel safety cage.

It all stacks up, doesn't it?

THE NEW VOLVO 940 ESTATE.

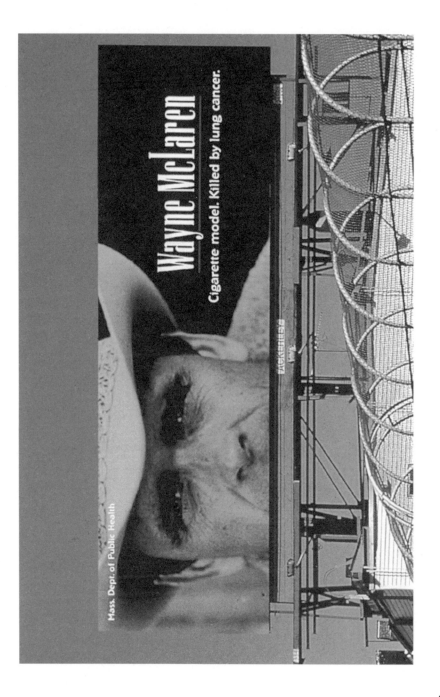

If you smoke, I smoke

Protect children. Don't make them breathe cigarette smoke. **NHS**

Visit www.givingupsmoking.co.uk or call 0800 169 0 169.

RULE SIX:
KEEP IT SIMPLE

Reductio ad absurdum.

Neil French, *The Copy Book*

Having satisfied the twin demands of relevance and objectivity, you will no doubt have a nice collection of ideas. You'll be wondering why they don't look like that really great idea that you wanted to end up with.

The reason may well be that your ideas are right-headed but not sufficiently simple. How do I know? Because 'simple' in ordinary life relates to something like, 'I've got some pine furniture for sale. It's well made and not expensive', which as a sentiment is simple because it is very easy to understand.

In advertising, as in design and as in marketing, 'simple' is a large rock falling from the sky and crushing your neighbour's house. It grabs your attention in a completely new way. Which event would you tell your friends about? Which would spur you into action? The comparison is ludicrously unfair because you're unlikely to be asked to publicize the end of the world, and if you were, it is clearly a better brief in the absolute sense than that for Stan's Pine Warehouse. However, the route to simplicity (Rule 6) is the key transition to make in order to move up from well-worded publicity to outstanding advertising. It's about changing the message into an event, a concept that Benetton, Playstation, Levis and a few other brave advertisers have grasped to their benefit. This chapter on simplicity provides the mental steel you need to throw away everything you've done so far in favour of something simpler and more powerful. It leads you to think brutal thoughts about your own work. A common one is to simply start again.

'Keep it simple' is easy enough to say. Indeed, if you were to ask anyone in advertising the golden rule, this is likely to be it. It's an admirable rule and the easiest way to use it is to check back when you have done your work to ask yourself, 'Is it simple?' However, simplicity is hard to achieve because you may very well make excuses for yourself. 'It's an awkward brief' or, 'It's what the client wants' are two common excuses used to explain over-complicated ads. People often simply don't realize how simple things can be, cutting back on the amount of body copy when perhaps the ad doesn't require copy at all.

One of the worst delusions is 'It's ok to produce a compli-cated message, I'm talking to intelligent people who can deal with complexity.' This is utterly the wrong mindset to have in advertising. The reason things need to be simple is not to cater for a notional class of stupid people. The need for simplicity is part of the craft, just as it would be for a designer of a flag or a pot. Have you ever looked at a simply designed vase and thought that it was all very well for the uneducated moron, but as an intelligent person you were more in the market for something fussy? Not often, hopefully.

The degree of simplicity in communications is not a targeting tool. It is the whole job. As G K Chesterton said, 'The simplification of anything is always sensational.'

There is a situation in which people of all kinds will appreciate a little detail and that is when they're interested. Consider the efforts of certain electrical retailers, who take out a double-page spread virtually every day of the week and simply publish all their prices. They even add fascinating extra nuggets of information such as what the prices were reduced from.

This level of detail is clearly not targeted at nuclear physicists, just as racing form guides aren't, nor the list prices of 10-year-old Fords. Detail clearly works for some retailers, not because they're aiming at boffins with nothing better to do than examine life's minutiae. The people they're talking to need to make very fine decisions based on cost. They have a strong desire for the product coupled with a strong need not to waste money. And while detail is key to their advertisements, in other ways the campaign, if you can call it that, is inexpressibly simple. These are our goods and these, our prices. If you don't get it, they'll be here again tomorrow and every day for eternity.

Another place you find the use of detail is on a television shopping channel, which itself is a digital-age version of a man on a market stall attracting an audience with a mixture of remorselessly detailed product demonstrations and low prices, usually expressed in a loud and grating voice. But there is a difference between detail and complexity.

No one would say that either the market stall-holder or the multimix presenter on the cable channel is guilty of over-complicating the issue. They are doing the job of a good copywriter. Getting the attention with an eye-grabbing demonstration then supplying an unbroken stream of further facts and reasons to buy, dosed with a little personal charm until the viewer is very nearly fascinated.

What they aren't doing is building a brand. The products are bit-part players in the branding of the channel, or the retailer, or the salesperson. At the market stall there's only one voice you hear and it isn't the voice of the 48-piece dinner service or the portable colour television.

To go back to the opening point, the easy way to use the golden rule is to look back at your work and say, 'Yes, that's a pretty simple piece of work, considering the client, the target market, and my own personal need to get home to watch the match.' However, as the above examples illustrate, the whole process needs to be geared to finding the one simple thing to say and to illustrating it with total clarity. If you are the writer at the end of this chain, you need to understand this, otherwise you tie yourself in knots trying to express convoluted briefs and redundant information in simple advertising.

At this point in the proceedings, it is unlikely that anyone who started reading with the view that the imposition of rules on this area is futile is still with us. But if there are one or two, good. This is where they will finally find themselves nodding. Rules such as 'Keep it simple' are most useful when everyone, not just the writer, knows about them. And the further up and down the chain these rules are known the better for all concerned.

There is a further distinction here to make between simple and simplistic. By that I mean that just because you have produced something simple does not make it good, for the obvious reason that it may be simple and unoriginal, simple and irrelevant or simple and boring. In those cases, simplicity isn't the problem, something else is.

Keeping it simple, then, is all about judgement. It's about being clear headed and ruthless enough to judge when your work is not good enough.

Be brutal. Let's say you've produced a poster for a local solicitors' firm. Ask yourself whether your poster would be intelligible to someone driving past at 40 miles per hour. If your answer is, 'How could it? It's for a solicitors' firm!' you've answered incorrectly. You have to be hypercritical.

Eschew surplusage.

Mark Twain

This quotation contains everything you need to know about the art of copywriting in the shortest possible number of words. Ultimately, keeping to this one can enact all the others:

- *Know your target – don't waste time speaking to the wrong people.*
- *Research – say only what is important.*
- *Answer the brief – don't waste time straying off-brief.*
- *Be relevant – get rid of everything irrelevant.*
- *Be objective – get rid of everything subjective.*
- *Keep it simple – avoid all complication.*
- *Know your medium – use the medium efficiently.*
- *Be ambitious – don't waste opportunities.*

The phrase 'eschew surplusage' is, as you've probably noticed, also an over-compressed form of words, which wittily reinforces the point. This in turn makes it easy to remember, and shows the value of originality and, not to put too fine a point on it, talent.

TWENTY THINGS TO AVOID

While you're getting there, it's instructive to consider what exactly it is that you need eschew. Here are 20 things to avoid.

1. Complicated tenses

Especially conditional and passive tenses. Write something as you feel it should be said, then try to convert it into simple, declarative language. Once you've done that, you may find that you're left with something very boring. If so, it can only be because the content is boring, so start again and say something interesting.

2. Complicated constructions

Embedded clauses (sentences within sentences) aren't against the rules, but even a slightly complex piece of embedding is probably better off as two separate sentences. Again, write it as you feel it should be said, then try breaking it into simpler components if necessary.

3. Stresses

If you must underline, use italics or bold letters for effect, the effect obviously isn't strong enough in what you've written alone. Exclamation marks, inverted commas and hyphens, where not demanded by grammar or convention, are probably being used lazily to imply tone of voice. Better to rewrite so you don't need them. Inverted commas in particular tend to look very weak when used in this way.

Why do standard letters from companies often pick a line out in bold? Does it mean the rest of the lines aren't important? If you think the important line might be lost, get rid of clutter to the point where you feel it will be read without being emboldened.

4. Clichés

Clichés are phrases people have heard many times before. Why say something that's been said before? There may be exceptions to the rule. A cliché may be poetic or apposite, have fallen into disuse or it may have some special character. It may introduce a note of familiarity into a difficult subject, but don't worry. Fair or unfair, kill as many clichés as you can. They are not an endangered species.

'A night to remember.' 'Family entertainment.' 'Go for a spin.' 'Up and down the country at this moment in time the winds of change are blowing.' They are everywhere and it's a good idea to kill as many as you can. It's always nicer to hear something you haven't heard before. If you can't say something without a cliché, there must be something wrong with what you are saying.

Clichés can of course be legitimately subverted. I mention this because so many people use subverted clichés when writing newspaper or newsletter headlines that it would be inhumane to imply this was bad practice, but tread warily. As with puns (see the section on humour in the next chapter), subverted or cleverly modified clichés are usually just poor jokes.

5. Mini clichés

Mini clichés are inevitable. They are small phrases of no particular distinction, but so useful that they are greatly overused, eg, 'on my way', 'as a matter of fact', 'here goes'. But compare these sentences:

The very occasional minor cliché can give a comfortable quality to a sharp, innovative piece of writing, but any more and it reads like mud.

One or two minor clichés can give a comfortable quality to take the edge off a sharp, innovative piece of writing, but any more and before you know it, it reads like mud.

The first one is clear of these mini clichés, the second has three. 'One or two' is comfy, 'take the edge off' is a bit wet, 'before you know it' is pure stodge.

6. Long words

The only reason for including a long or little known word should be where absolute precision of meaning is vital. If the audience doesn't know the word, what's the point of being precise about the meaning? It's surprising how long words cumulatively spoil the apparent simplicity of a sentence, or the timing and delivery of a line of dialogue.

Adopt a habit: every time you come across a long or fancy word in your writing, spend 15–30 seconds searching your brain for a one-syllable version. For example, even when I used 'the very occasional minor cliché' above, a moment's thought could have shortened it to 'the odd minor cliché'.

(Obviously when detecting these unnecessarily long words your sensitivity may be adjusted a little according to your audience. But not much.)

7. '-ing' words

'-ing' words are bad. They're not very bad, but it's worth it to keep an eye on them. The one syllable they add to a word combines with the extra layer of complexity they usually bring to make them a valid target.

Compare these sentences:

This is part of the thinking behind avoiding '-ing' words, as it's surprising how using them can make writing unexciting.

This is why you should avoid '-ing' words. They gum up your sentences.

There's not a great difference between them in normal writing situations, but usually, if you're a copywriter, you're not in a normal situation. You may, for example, be writing for an actor to perform. If you were an actor, which of the example sentences would you rather perform in front of a thousand people? Which could you put more emotion into?

8. Dull words

Try to use active, exciting words. It's another way of passing more information in a short space. It's not that words like 'went' or 'cut' are that boring, but it misses the opportunity to say much about how a person went or cut. 'Slid', 'bounced', 'waddled', 'jetted', etc tell you more about a person than 'went'; and 'hack', 'dissect', 'bite', 'saw', etc tell you more about an action than 'cut'. By putting information there you may be able to leave it out elsewhere. Tony

Antin, in *Great Print Advertising,* has a tip for headlines which is to arrange your line so that the most interesting words are at the beginning. This isn't, however, an excuse for floweriness. Which brings us to…

9. Showing off your talent

What you say should be so interesting that the reader/viewer/ listener is not aware of the cleverness of the writer. It's true of most great ads. They work like machines, and appear to be written by machines. This is no coincidence. They often come from very well run organizations.

Flowery or over-written scripts are particularly bad if they are, like ads, intended for frequent repetition.

10. Showing off your knowledge

This is possibly an even more serious crime, at least in advertising. If you are writing dutifully on behalf of your client it is to be expected that your talent will show through accidentally to those who recognize such things. But any display of knowledge other than of the product, accidental or otherwise, is undesirable. Even using such words as 'obviously' indicate that what follows is obvious to the writer when it may not be to a reader. At the other end of the scale, a lapse into mannered use of Latin or French is the worst kind of pomposity in an advertisement, and should only be considered if your target market wears some kind of crown. (*The Economist* can be forgiven its recent poster headline 'Carpe Annum' however.)

11. Those things you do

Most people have writing habits that show up in the use of certain words and phrases. These words and phrases are likely to be perfectly acceptable in themselves, but may be evidence of a personal style that is undesirable. From the consumer's point of view the copywriter does not exist. The ad is a communication between them and the company concerned. Some of the great creatives do have personal styles that meld with that of the companies they become most associated with, but that is a genuine relationship, where they become the voice of a company in the same way as does that company's CEO or Managing Director. But unless you, like Richard Branson, are the voice of the company, go with Bob Levinson, who said on this subject:

The writer who attempts to put his agency's mark on the client's copy or – God forbid – his own mark should pay with his job. And his severance should be that of his writing hand.

12. Bad dialogue

Avoid the following:

- *Names. For some reason, when people first write dialogue, their characters constantly name each other in every line. It doesn't sound as natural as you think and it isn't always necessary to name people at all.*
- *Long speeches. Break up long speeches with short replies from others.*
- *Children. Don't give them adult words and sentiments to say.*
- *Directions. As with exclamation marks and underlining in prose, you shouldn't need directions in scripts. If you think you do need them, something's wrong. Such things as character, delivery and emotional state should be self-evident. If not, rewrite. Consider the pointlessness of the direction:*

Hamlet: (reflectively) To be, or not to be, that is the question.

If you wish to create a naturalistic effect in dialogue, try to observe the way real people talk. Record a conversation and transcribe it. See how pregnant the words are with information about those talking, their state of mind, their personalities and their relationship with the person they're talking to. Read your own script out loud. Are your words as rich with information? Or do you hear just your own voice trying to bring the subject round to the product in an awkward fashion? The goal is not to copy real speech, but once again to use word choice to pass more information about the person speaking.

13. Words and sentences

Avoid these. Actions speak louder. See your job not as a writer of words, but as an avoider of words. Adopt the habit of chopping something out completely if it isn't working. Not as your last resort, but your first. Even if it is working, try cutting it out; it may improve things. People don't wait for a full stop to stop reading. If they're bored they'll turn the page or flip channels after a few words. Get to the point. Once you've made it, finish, or make another one.

'Kill your darlings' is a well-known saying, apparently, in writing circles. The idea is that if you find you are personally in love with a joke, word or a line, a warning bell should go off in your head, to say cut it out and replace it with something better, or leave the hole. Maybe the joke, word, line was implied anyway. Maybe it changes the tone of the piece too much. It's strange, but it works, if only because it forces you to be hypercritical.

14. Abstract words

If you must have words, keep them as concrete as possible. It's just simpler to read about dogs, cats, plants, cheese, socks and the world of solid things than it is to read about suspicion, care, imperturbability and germination.

15. Mistakes

Don't make them at all. Get used to rereading what you write purely for grammar and punctuation. Check spelling with patience. Sometimes when you've got a hangover, any word can look odd. Don't be too proud to look it up or to ask someone where a comma goes.

You can take certain liberties with grammar where there are positive benefits for comprehension. Advertising has championed the verb-less sentence. Like this one. To the purist, they represent what is wrong with advertising copy, but all these liberties are only taken in the interests of reader-friendliness. You mustn't think they're mandatory. Don't break the rules of grammar for the sake of it or, even worse, to make something read like an ad.

People often start writing copy by mimicking ads they've read before and churn out verb-less sentences, subject-less sentences, sentences beginning with 'and' or 'because'. It can be horrible. In comparison, it's far better to be a purist. If you feel it's lowering your high writing standards to break rules, don't do it. Grammatical writing doesn't have to be dull. After all, the rules of grammar are there for reader-friendliness in the first place. Don't forget that people read far faster than you write, so what you write as a deftly phrased, three-word, verb-less sentence can completely lose its meaning when read at full tilt. The guarantee of a grammatical sentence is that it is self-contained, so your reader needn't wonder what part of the previous sentence it refers to.

If you do employ a little grammar-perversion, make sure you reread it several times, coming to it cold as often as possible, so that you know it doesn't trip up your reader.

16. Sloppy layout

Avoid your copy or script looking ugly or unstructured on the page. This especially applies to scripts. Whatever the conventions are in your organization for margins, column size for scripts, underlining of headings, number of spaces between character name and corresponding line of dialogue on scripts, justification, use of full stops in headlines and so on, keep to them. If your work is being typed for you, being a perfectionist may cause friction, but there's one way round it. Do it yourself.

Your script or piece of copy should be a polished diamond on the page. It should be easy to understand and easy to use as a working document for actors and presenters. Even if it's going no further than your department head, immaculate presentation deters changes and misunderstandings. If you don't know what your layout conventions are, find out. If there are none, here's a general rule. Don't cram your writing up too tight. Airy line-breaks and wide margins make things easy to digest for a reader who may be stressed, ignorant, not concentrating, or drunk. (It's possible.) They also leave room for legible marks and comments by those who use your copy, such as actors, directors, typesetters, clients, sound engineers and many more.

17. Unintentional repetition

In press copy, avoid using the same word too often in the same piece, especially within the same paragraph. 'And's and 'if's don't count. And intentional repetitions don't count, as in the use of 'count' in the sentence you're reading now. But most words do count. It's amazing how tawdry it is to repeat a word like 'however' within four lines of saying it the first time. If it's not intentional, it's sloppy.

In dialogue, however, repetition is a valuable tool:

John: It's amazing how tawdry it is to repeat a word like 'however'.
Jane: I wouldn't say 'however' in the first place.
John: What would you say?

Jane: I'd say 'nevertheless'.
John: I wouldn't say that.
Jane: Wouldn't you?
John: No.

Ok, it's not Alan Ayckbourn. But the repetition of 'however', 'say', and 'would' creates a sensation of flow in the speech, even though it isn't realistic. Realism is not as desirable as you'd expect. Normal speech isn't constructed to put across beautifully simple ideas with ingenious clarity, so it's not always helpful to copy normal speech rhythms.

Some intentional repetitions could bear some scrutiny too. The technique of mindless repetition to make people remember what you're saying is crude, and not as good as having a memorable idea.

18. Adjectives

Even adjectives can spoil the tone of straight-talking copy. If you're advertising something, of course you're going to speak highly of it, so it sounds hollow to say it's great, or tasty. It just sounds like boasting. Adjectives can be difficult to avoid, as the whole point of most copywriting is effectively to boast about a product. But it's better to say 'Wipe-easy Toilet Rolls have a smell of pine,' than 'Wipe-easy Toilet Rolls have a heavenly smell of pine.' One sounds like a selling point, the other, a sales pitch. Even when they're not pitch-type adjectives, chop them out anyway. It might help. If it doesn't, you can always put them back again.

19. Ambiguity

Once the grammar is simple and everything is perfect, don't forget semantics:

John went to see the teacher in a wheelchair.

Everything is simple, but who's in the wheelchair? Even if you think it's obvious from the context, iron out the ambiguities. A moment's confusion for the reader may not be disastrous, but it's very lazy on your part. Unlike some of the above, ambiguity is utterly avoidable.

20. These words

- *Expertise.*
- *Value.*
- *Incredible.*
- *Look!*
- *Quality.*
- *Bonanza.*
- *Second-to-none.*
- *Giveaway.*

There are many others. They usually add nothing to an ad apart from a cheap glaze.

Simplicity, in conclusion, is an end in itself. You can enjoy an act of simplicity as much as a good joke, as these examples show:

It Works Better.
It Costs Less.
End Of Ad.

© 1990 CIBA-GEIGY Corporation, Turf and Ornamental Products, Box 18300, Greensboro, NC 27419. Always read and follow label directions.

RULE SEVEN: KNOW YOUR MEDIUM

Advertising is the greatest art form of the 20th Century
Marshall McLuhan, *Advertising Age*, 1976

Rule 7 is essentially about technique. One hears occasionally of how an advertising creative person's vast salary may be justified by their ability to sprinkle magic dust over the finished product. In other words they can take a thought or an advertising idea and reshape it to give it qualities that make it leap off the page, or grab your attention when it's shown in a commercial break. Nigel Rose, who is both writer and art director of the now famous Wonderbra poster, 'Hello Boys', spoke of making an ad 'pop' – a change of vocabulary or of word order, the removing of a border or of a superfluous design element.

The magical power that such people possess is actually only experience. But it's a particular experience and an understanding of the way each individual medium works. It's not merely about applying the final polish but about knowing the medium. About the microscopic subtleties of typography, how different inks behave on newsprint, what may and may not be done with retouching. This chapter comprises a few rules of this kind, though for the copywriter rather than the art director. These may stand in for experience while you acquire your own opinions and techniques for the various media in which you work.

From the previous chapter you may have gained the impression that to succeed in advertising you need to throw away your fine craftsman's tools and replace them with pile drivers and mallets. Don't. In a way all communication works like a radio transmission, which combines a powerful radio signal strong enough to reach a large audience, with minute variations, which carry the detail of the message. It's the same with speech, where we have the powerful machine of the language on which we superimpose minute subtleties of tone and inflexion. You need a powerful medium such as posters or TV acting as a carrier for the perfect expression of your proposition. To best utilize the qualities of each medium, you need to know a little of its subtleties.

Five per cent of finding out about your medium is, of course, part of the research you must do before starting. But that is only a minimum requirement. You should be able to aspire higher than just producing work that is technically broadcastable. To excel, in the way that every ad needs to if it is to get noticed, you need a more advanced knowledge. It would seem appropriate to start with radio.

RADIO

This is a medium in which the general immersion you experience as a listener in the car or wherever, can actually be harmful to the appreciation of the possibilities.

There is a great temptation to add to the noise with more of the same. This is more difficult to address than in the press. For instance, to see how an ad can look different to those in a motoring magazine you only have to look at non-motoring magazines.

With radio, you don't really have much to compare. Yes, there are other radio stations, but there is a sameness of delivery across many radio stations, which is even more pronounced when you limit yourself to just comparing the commercials on these different stations. More voices ranting about products, more catchy music. You need to find sounds that can stand for your client's product or service, and that alone, wherever on the wavebands they're heard.

For the writer, perhaps the worst thing you can do is write too much. Unless it's an announcement of national importance, people won't really care. Far better to hack back on words mercilessly. (Be honest when you time your script. If you really can't read it slowly in your allotted time, cut until you can.) Leave only the kernel of what is being said. If the kernel isn't interesting enough, ditch it.

Radio is strangely intimate. If you're whispering in people's ears, simple things work better than bragging rambles or convoluted situation comedy. Create silences or surprising sound textures. Short simple lines allow the speaker to give just the right performance because they allow pauses and scope for more character in the intonation.

Radio is the most natural form of communication. If you want to tell your friend something, you don't send him a 48-sheet poster, you ring him up and tell him aurally.

Paul Burke, copywriter

Think of ideas that use the fact that you can hear but not see. Carling Black Label produced an excellent radio commercial in which a man is told to empty his pockets in a police station. There followed 20 seconds of sound effects as metal objects, beds, crockery, etc fall out on to the desk. After a pause a policeman says, 'Come on. And the other one.' The noises start again as another policeman says, 'I bet he drinks Carling Black Label'.

The idea could only work on radio, and has the other virtue of having more sound effects than words.

Remember to treat the production of a radio ad seriously. Don't skip research. Cast it thoroughly and invest your characters with believable personalities. Don't always use humour. Try touching a nerve. Integrate the product skilfully, or make it integral to the idea so it doesn't blow the whole tone when it turns up.

POSTERS

Posters are the purist's advertising medium. Placed out in the real world, with room for only six words or less, it's a great medium to use in original ways. For example, there was a poster for Budgie food in South America, which was covered in birds all day because the agency had placed some of the bird food on a ledge under the poster.

Another example is the Acupuncture clinic in Kensington that advertised itself with a 48-sheet poster showing a map of the area. Sticking into the poster was a giant pin showing the location of the clinic. Another is the GLC poster which asked what would happen when Whitehall ran London, with the poster wrapped in red tape.

It's arguable that all great ads are to some extent a great use of the medium. You may be forgiven for thinking that posters need no researching as a medium. Broadly speaking, it's true that you hardly need to go and see what a poster site looks like before putting pen to paper, as you pass posters every day. Nevertheless, once or twice while you're walking along a street, it's worth just stopping and looking at a poster site anew. Look how people walk by the craziest, brightest coloured poster site as if it wasn't there. People are not going to write to *The Times* reporting an unusual coloured immensity by the side of a road in their town.

Advertising is no longer a new phenomenon. Look at photographs of Victorian London. Every surface seems to be covered with advertising hoardings. The advertisements themselves

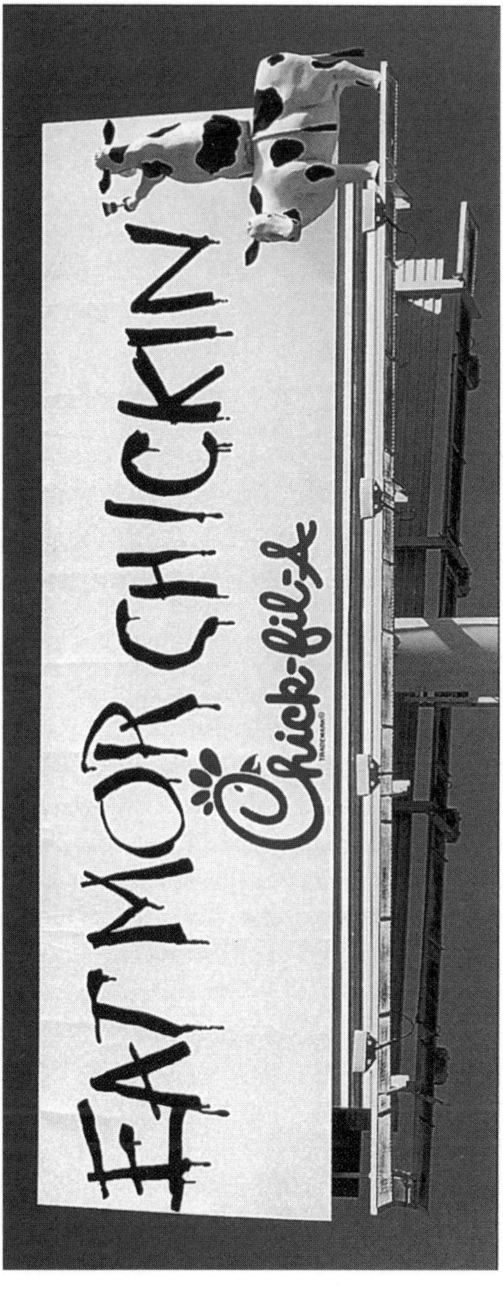
EAT MOR CHICKIN
Chick-fil-A

make outrageous claims for ridiculous waxes, potions and brass implements, yet even 100 years ago, no one in the pictures looks up in astonishment or struggles to control their horses. It's not enough to rely on the size and position of posters for your impact. It's a good exercise to write down your ideas for posters as sketches about the size of a matchbox to get some idea of whether they are simple and graphic enough in their look, and intriguing enough in their subject, to draw attention.

Posters also have a special quality through being visible not just to your target market, but to everyone. They can spread your appeal at the same time as talking to your current users.

PRESS COPY

There will be moments of course when the idea is sold, the photography done and the headline set, when someone will ask you to write copy.

Press copy, to some copywriters, is special. It's an advertising craft that isn't briefed out to an illustrator, photographer or director for realization, but which uses the copywriter's own talents directly on to the page.

The special nature of the press is partly due to the perfect platform a newspaper offers for intelligent communication of product information or the ultimate presentation of campaigning arguments, and partly because so many great copywriters have gone before to set the standards. It's an area where less isn't always more. Very occasionally long copy is permissible. For example, to some readers 5000 words on the quality of a Macadamia nut may be strangely fascinating where 25 words may not. It's interesting to think that there could be undiscovered depths to a nut. In comparison, a nut ad sporting only 25 words will confirm your worst suspicions.

Long copy press opportunities are sadly rare; they depend on a confluence of circumstances. The people with enough money to pay for such an ad are rarely the ones whose product would merit 5000 words. Computers, banks and cars frequently use the press, but don't always have enough to say that will fascinate, while the sex lives of chimpanzees have no commercial dimension. The opportunities do still exist, however, and their rarity does contribute to a sense of event when a long copy press ad does appear.

Another caveat to bear in mind is this. Just because your *New York Times* or *Daily Telegraph* doesn't seem to have changed much in 50 years, the world, and therefore the reader, has. They have far more demands on their attention then ever, and even if they are attracted by your ad through its brilliant, intelligent simplicity, they are not disposed to read your copy by way of a reward to you. Any rewards going should be in favour of the reader. They're driving down the motorway of their day; you must entice them off on to your little dirt track with a few very, very enticing opening words. And if you don't keep the reward or the promise of reward going throughout the copy, they'll be back on the motorway without a backward glance. As they are quite prepared to quit in mid sentence if necessary, it can be quite difficult to slip in a reference to your fluff-removing gadget or bland insurance service without losing them. Particularly as elsewhere in the newspaper, perhaps on the same page, there's a world war developing. So, what to do?

You are aiming for flow. One idea should flow into the next as if it were the most natural thing. Intense writing and rewriting achieves this. Flesh it out, cut it back, flesh it out again, cut it back again. Change the order of the points several times. Find out what works best. Find a central thread. Be prepared to abandon all if another central thread occurs to you. Hack out the clichés, straighten out the complex sentences. Make sure ideas still flow naturally into one another. Chop out your favourite gag, perhaps.

And serve. It should read like a drop of water sliding down a wall. A light, but unstoppable descent towards the final thought. If the reading snags anywhere, iron out the offending sentence, then read it again. There should be no point at which the reader is put off.

Adrian Holmes advocates a simple method. Before starting your copy, work out where it will end. Creating the flow of logic is similar to the job of erecting a telephone line from A to B, in that you can't very well put the wire up without the poles.

One novelist said he disciplined himself by thinking, as he sat down to write, of being on a stage, in front of hundreds of people just as the doors to the bar are opened at the back of the hall. His job was to keep everybody in their seats by words alone. If you have mental discipline like this, you shouldn't need many rules. You'd use them anyway in order to achieve the effect you want.

Linking

To achieve the flow described above, it may help to think of it as linking:

- *The first line should make you want to read the second.*
- *The second line should pick up a word or idea from the first and lob it sweetly into the third.*
- *The third should continue the process.*
- *The process shouldn't become mechanical.*

An easy way to link is to use linking words or phrases, as in the following:

Linking words are useful.
Indeed, at the start of a sentence they create the illusion of natural flow.
Of course, some short phrases perform exactly the same function.
However, they shouldn't be used too often.
After all, it's one of the things that can make advertising copy irritating.

Have you ever written on a banana in biro? It's crazy but it works like a dream. You wish all writing could be this way. It's smooth. It flows. It's sensually worded. A strongly worded letter of complaint; sonnets; odes to lilies that everything can be improved. That even the familiar can be looked at in a new knowledge. It makes you realise. And that imagination is more powerful than HONDA. You get the urge to write poems;

Do you believe in the power of dreams?

GOLFING AND VOLVO:

THE

IRREFUTABLE LINKS.

1 'THE GREEN' IS A GOLFING TERM. SOME VOLVOS ARE GREEN.

2 A DRIVER IS ESSENTIAL FOR A GOLF BALL ON A TEE. LIKEWISE FOR A MOVING VOLVO.

3 GOLF: ONE O, ONE L. NEXT TO EACH OTHER. VOLVO: ONE O, ONE L. NEXT TO EACH OTHER. (AND ANOTHER O.)

4 A VOLVO HAS FOUR WHEELS. A GOLF TROLLEY HAS TWO WHEELS. DO YOU NOTICE AN 'EVEN NUMBER' PATTERN EMERGING?

5 YOU PUTT BALLS IN GOLF. YOU CAN PUT BALLS IN A VOLVO.

6 YOU USE THE TERM 'BIRDIE' IN GOLF. DRIVE PAST AN AVIARY IN A VOLVO, AND IT'S LIKE DEJA-VU.

7 GOLF SHAFTS USE VARIOUS ALUMINIUM ALLOYS. EVER NOTICED A VOLVO'S WHEEL-RIMS? SAY NO MORE.

8 WIN AT GOLF AND YOU CAN BE A CUP HOLDER. DRIVE A VOLVO AND YOU CAN HAVE A CUP HOLDER.

9 COMPARE A VOLVO AERIAL WITH A GOLF FLAGPOLE. DO THE WORDS 'CYLINDRICAL' AND 'SHAPE' SPRING TO MIND?

10 TIGER WOODS PLAYS GOLF. DEREK WOODS IS, NOT A WORD OF A LIE, REGIONAL MANAGER FOR VOLVO MIDLANDS.

VOLVO
for life

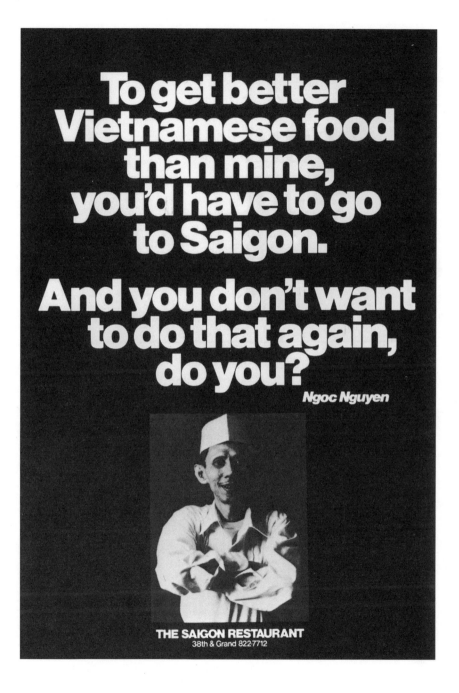

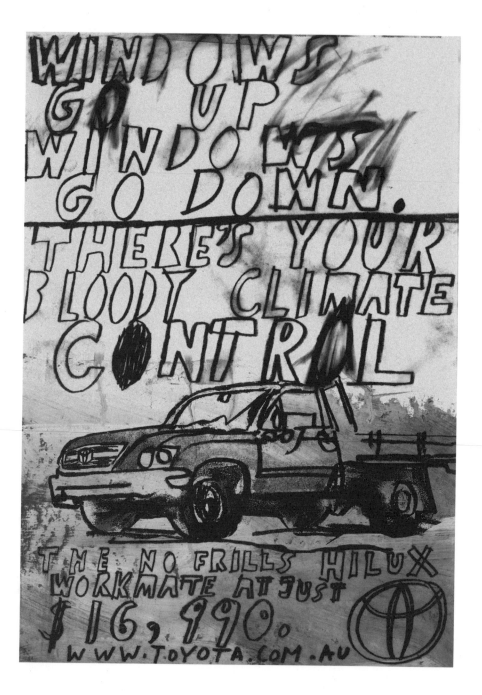

It's OK to aim for a reading age of 12, but it shouldn't mean your copy reads as though it was written by a 12-year-old.

Don't write as if you have a gun at your head. Relax. Be prepared to throw in an aside, use brackets and appropriate quotes. Be original. Remember the wit of 'eschew surplusage'. Exemplify the content of your message through its form.

Don't be overly formal. Just because your client is rich and powerful, it doesn't mean he or she can't speak with a human voice. In written material, speech mannerisms can be, well, quite refreshing.

Humour

Likewise, be funny. Or wry, or dry, or whatever's appropriate. An advertisement is important to the advertiser because so many salaries depend on its success. But to the audience it's just another cry for attention. Humour often works because it gets over this barrier. If nothing else it's an instant reward for reading the ad.

But this has to be judged correctly. Many writers get into the habit of thinking humour is right for every client, until the day they hear, 'I'm surprised you find the recalling of several thousand of our products as a subject for comedy', and make a mental note to ration the gags in future.

So, by all means, use humour, so long as it's used in the right place. There is also one more caveat. Make sure you're as funny as you think you are. If you're not sure, try this simple test. When you give the copy to someone else to read, they laugh. Or at least smile. If people don't laugh or smile, you can't be sure it's funny, and you need to be. It may still be funny if nobody laughs; it may be wry humour. On the other hand, it may be pathetic. You can't tell. But if they laugh, it's funny.

Don't put too many funny lines in a piece of copy. It can read as a desperate bid for approval. If anyone is reading (a big if, remember) they will be reading because they're interested in your facts.

Generally, avoid puns. The few good ones don't really justify the misery caused by the rest. Puns are much misunderstood, though. The trouble is that the word 'pun' suggests a small-minded play on words for the simple reason that most puns are. But really, the area of wordplay is far richer. Puns go from awful down to worse. But they also go upwards into an area where puns aren't jokes, but a way of contracting a lot of information into a very few words.

'Labour isn't working' is arguably this country's most famous poster, used in 1979 to help the UK Conservative Party into power for an 18-year stay. It's wheeled out every election for one excuse or another. Accompanied by a picture of a dole queue, the headline means the country's workforce has nothing to do. It's a pun, but it's not an awful one because the Labour Party obviously chose the word 'Labour' to reflect the interests of the workforce. It's a pointed way of saying that Labour was failing at the very thing it stood for. On the basis of that, even if you liked Labour, what remaining point was there in voting for them?

It's a pun that changed history. Its writer, Andrew Rutherford, once challenged me to name a single great ad that relied on a pun. I couldn't think of one, perhaps because the word 'pun' suggests 'puny'. His poster certainly wasn't.

More on press copy

All this style and flow is secondary to information. Don't throw out a fact for a piece of flow. Ideally, flow really isn't about elegant linking phrases, it's about finding the natural flow of your information. If it's created only with linking words and the like, you'll find the end result strangely artificial. When it's an apparently natural flow of ideas the effect is more persuasive and less like a salesperson's patter.

While on this subject, I should pass on one of the best copywriting tips ever devised. It's from David Abbot (though sometimes attributed to others) who said that he often checked how convincing his copy was by reading it out aloud in a corny American voice. If the sense survived this kind of treatment, it maybe had a chance of persuading readers. In reality, a long piece of copy is just a sales spiel as hard and as mercenary as any other sales spiel, regardless of the aura of old-school craftsmanship that surrounds it. The only difference is that without a salesperson present, the ever-present grin has to be represented in the copy by a certain stylistic charm.

When you can get the flow of information right it seems perfectly obvious, but you have to work hard in order to achieve it. If it reads easy, it wrote hard. Experiment with the order of your points over and over again until it suddenly looks as though you wrote it off the top of your head.

Give your copy an engine. Copy should have an overall shape. It's not a bad habit to end a piece by returning in some elegant way to the opening thought. It's good if your opening is not obvious in the way it's expressed. Maybe a short sentence of only three to eight words.

How about a question?

Better still, if the subject allows, try to take the opening concept or idea right through to the end.

All press ads should dominate the page on which they appear. The worst crime of all press advertising is to use an expensive double page spread, which readers immediately flick past because there is no editorial.

NEW MEDIA

'New media' is an alluring phrase holding out the prospect of billion pound industries created with a press conference, a text message and a very rude video.

Dismissive as this sounds there is something in it. A little smart thinking in the new media area may not lead to immediate unthinkable wealth, but it may earn the equivalent public attention of a million pound traditional media spend.

The reason is that there is a wonderful fluidity about how new, technology-driven media interlink. One of the most exciting facets of this changing landscape is that, unlike conventional media, where the agency or client simply points at the media package they want and utters 'buy', new media is at a stage where it can still be defined through usage.

An example that sticks in the mind, not necessarily for the right reasons, is an idea by TBWA on behalf of its Labour Party client in the 2005 elections. I referred positively to the strategy behind this campaign in the Introduction, but it had its less exalted moments.

It has become a norm in British elections for parties with a dwindling war chest to use a new medium of their own to get a message across and keep in the public eye. The poster unveiling is one such. The leader of the party turns up at a prearranged place such as a car park in a marginal constituency with a pack of journalists and an invited group of members of the public, probably party workers. They unveil a hitherto unseen poster and get its punchy message on the evening news without going to the bother of having to roll out the poster on sites around the country.

TBWA refined this. They created half a dozen posters and put them on the party website so that members could vote on their preference. These were billed as concepts rather than finished ads on the basis that not all would go forward, so they were crude in execution, showing the opposition leaders usually rather compromised in their juxtaposition with rough graphic images. But two were crude in another way. One showed the leader of the opposition Conservative Party Michael Howard as a Jewish pawnbroker swinging a gold watch, and the other placed the heads of the leader and his deputy on the bodies of cartoon pigs.

The anti-Semitism of the images was claimed to be a figment in the minds of those that complained about it, and in any case these innocent, fun-loving images were not published as public communications but as a private competition or even research.

The news coverage was on an enormous scale. The messages were broadcast at a tiny cost and to a massive effect, entirely due to the offence caused by the crude images. Is this a viral campaign? It worked like one. But on closer inspection it was really a spot of internal research, which not only isn't new, it isn't even media.

So these taboo-breaking images could be broadcast safe in the knowledge that the drawbridge could be pulled up afterwards. If anyone complains (and they did) this wasn't intentionally offensive, it was being researched, it was something the agency did, agencies are not politicians so wouldn't have been aware of the sensitivities and so on.

This shows both the possibilities of new media and one danger. The way a humble piece of research germinated at lightning speed into an internet, media and political event, all at a tiny cost, is a powerful demonstration of what new media can do.

But think of what the message was of those two posters in particular and you can see that where new media is internet-based, part of its power comes from its ability to do commerce in the sleazier areas of human motivation. The innocence claimed for these images is entirely illusory. Agencies spend careful hours deciding exactly what goes into a poster and considering what might be taken out by the viewer. Posters that point out to an electorate that the Conservative Party happens to have a Jewish leadership simply cannot happen by accident. And the more you think about that little nugget, the worse it gets.

New variant

There are two kinds of new media. There are those that are old media that have gained more currency or power by new technology, or just that have become more fashionable by means of better usage or improved technology. Then there are media the like of which no human has hitherto set eyes upon. This is my personal taxonomy but I believe it the healthiest way to view the subject. For example, floor panels (ads on the floors of supermarkets) are new media. They are also the result of some new technology: the new glues available leave no residue so that means that the panels are more appealing to the shop keeper, and they can be taken up at the end of a promotion, which is more appealing to customers. There are TVs entertaining Post Office queues with tailored content and barking out '3 for 2' offers over garage forecourts. There are bus stop 'adshel' posters that can talk to you, beam information to your mobile or change their image at night. Poster companies are careful not to turn down the possibility of posting an advertisement anywhere.

These are neither to get excited about nor sneezed at. The improvement in the mechanics of how floor tiles work or the ability of a bus stop poster to talk really does give you opportunities creatively. The Art Director Richard Evans took advantage of the new technology to create a poster for Sci-Fi Channel in which disembodied voices struck up a banal conversation at a bus stop. It forced those waiting to take a sudden interest in the adshel poster next to them advertising the movie 'The Invisible Man'. The can-do attitude of poster companies is worth knowing too. Without it the *Economist* poster shown earlier, posted on the top of a bus addressing readers in high office, would not have happened. But both those examples are around 10 years old, so clearly newness isn't the most interesting part of this story.

With the possible exception of the technology that allows information to be beamed to your phone, these new applications or new facilities of existing media work in the same way as old media. They are self-contained.

The second category, media the like of which no human has ever set eyes upon, is a set of disparate media that have an astonishing potential because the technology on which they are based is not of the sort that addresses you from afar, but is itself communicative. A TV commercial presents itself as a little show in your living room. When it has finished it picks up its hat, counts the pennies and shuffles off. Likewise radio and cinema. A poster tries frenetically to get your attention from a hoarding as you go to work. Press ads try to lure you into their world with something like a low price or pretty face, but their role in your life is swiftly guillotined with a turn of the page.

New media (second category) is a new form of advertising that is best exemplified with what has come to be termed 'viral'. There is no standard way to run viral campaigns. Often they just happen. A director shoots a film that goes beyond the usual bounds of taste and TV advertising censorship laws. It's posted on the internet or e-mailed to a group of friends. People talk about it, gather round each other's computers with hands over mouths, then peel away saying, 'Send it to me.'

A text message from a gaming software company leads you to advertisements cunningly disguised as cool stuff on a specially created website. A piece of direct mail contains nothing but a web address and a spoon. An e-mail arrives from someone you know and respect, containing a film about a car with your name suddenly appearing halfway through. A dancing animal becomes an international star by means of e-mail and somehow you end up downloading the music.

Like a virus the form seems to have an ability to mutate to fit the content, the audience and the context. Thus the Labour Party Flying Pigs poster may have been old media in principle, but became new media as its fame spread. It spread in terms of the numbers who knew of it, but also the kind of coverage it got.

That is significant if you are considering putting a little viral campaign into your mix. There is no rate card, no 'opportunity to see' figure. You've heard of the expression 'The media is the message'. New Media (variant B) exemplifies a new principle, that the message is the media. You can't take your sweet little commercial with your packshot on the end and expect it to be broadcast round the world. Nor can you expect to send any old pornography round and have it reflect well on your company's proud name.

A good little motto from elsewhere in this book is 'Don't write words, write events.' This is exactly how to approach viral. The medium you choose may not be the medium you end up in.

Virgin Mobile's campaign featuring the line, 'The devil makes work for idle thumbs' is a case where a company and an agency have got to grips with using new media intelligently. The conventional media manifestation of this line was a TV campaign showing beautifully made, and slightly unsettling scenes where a bored fellow fiddles with some knobs and gets himself in an unpleasant scrape as a result. It seemed a roundabout way to drive a 3p per minute text tariff into people's minds. But these weren't ordinary people, these were young people, for it is they who text the most. For a relative grown up it seemed slightly obscure. One was supposed to extrapolate from the remote danger inherent in not having enough to do with your thumbs that one had better get onto this low-priced tariff to avoid such eventualities. But these commercials were the tip of a media iceberg, the bulk of which was a viral campaign of bizarre films exchanged like football cards over the net, films that hairy-nosed 40-somethings like me had no inkling of. 'The devil makes work for idle thumbs' didn't intend to wind up in Endline Café with all the brand statements. It was doing something else, something that made the 3p tariff for which it spoke, culty and cool. It was viral and it worked, because the young people who text are the same young people who love clever, dark, elusive happenings in cyberspace. They lapped up the campaign in all its manifestations, and young thumbs were rarely idle as a result.

TELEVISION

Rules are weaker in the area of TV advertising because of the value of originality. To foul up can actually produce an end product that looks very fresh and attracts the attention, albeit in the way a car crash does. The only downside may be its effect on your reputation. If you wish to make a career out of cool mastery of TV as a medium, it may be wise to keep to the general rules expressed earlier, those of simplicity, of relevance, of knowing who you're talking to and so on. It is a very naked medium for your mistakes so I would recommend spending as long on your script as possible. Make sure you really have made the idea simple, that any dialogue really is natural. It will show up horribly if your script isn't up to it.

The good news is that you are very rarely alone when you make TV commercials. Be prepared to listen and make judicious choices of people to work with. The most valuable one to get right is often the director. Find one who knows about advertising ideas and you're in good hands. Beyond this, accumulate as much TV experience as you can because it's not only valuable but also enjoyable.

The only rule that might be of any value in the area of TV advertising is this: don't underestimate what it can achieve. Some say that all great brands are created on TV, though as we have seen, new media can be pretty good too. But for sheer scale and depth of penetration into people's lives, you can't, for the moment, beat telly.

For example, when Lyndon Johnson ran for re-election as US President in 1964, Doyle Dane Bernbach was asked to make a TV commercial in support of his campaign. The election happened a year after Kennedy was assassinated and against the background of the Vietnam War. Johnson's Republican opponent was Barry Goldwater, whose political outlook may be best explained in his own words, used in his 1964 nomination acceptance speech: 'I would remind you that extremism in the defence of liberty is no vice.'

The commercial, produced in cooperation with Bill Moyers of the Democratic campaign team, showed a girl in a field picking petals off a daisy and counting from one to ten. This image was intercut with a nuclear missile on a launch pad as a male voice counted down from ten to one. There followed a nuclear explosion and the voice of Lyndon Johnson himself, as he delivered conceivably the most powerful piece of copy ever written:

These are the stakes. To make a world in which all of God's children can live. Or to go into the dark. We must either love each other, or we must die.

The commercial ends:

Vote for President Johnson on November 3. The stakes are too high for you to stay home.

This was an oversimplification of the issues in that election, but it was an oversimplification shown at prime time on NBC at the point in history when it mattered most. It set the agenda and prosecuted the argument in a way that was unmissable and made you want to act. It may even be argued that it changed history. Goldwater said of the Daisy commercial, 'There was no doubt as to the meaning: Barry Goldwater would blow up the world if he became President of the United States.' Lyndon Johnson won the election by 486 electoral votes to 52.

'Daisy' is interesting for several reasons. One is that the context in which an ad appears is vital to its effect. Another is that it wasn't afraid to be unpopular. When Lyndon Johnson heard of the complaints of unfairness he asked to book more airtime. The most significant thing is that it doesn't attempt to do too much, to cover a broad range of policies, as most party political broadcasts seem to. It finds the jugular issue and goes for it.

Compare 'Daisy' to another political advertisement aired around 30 years later for the Labour Party in Britain. It was the party's first attempt to employ advertising techniques and therefore evinces a common layman's view of what advertising techniques are. The party leader, Neil Kinnock, is shown walking along a cliff top, his bald head gleaming in the sunlight as a voiceover speaks of vision and resolve. In other words, this is a normal party political broadcast with the addition of some soft focus imagery. It was actually reasonably popular at the time, but today it's impossible to recall a single policy or idea from that broadcast.

What made 'Daisy' an ad rather than a piece of imagery was its logic, which went something like this:

- *Nuclear weapons cause unimaginable devastation.*
- *The president controls the country's nuclear weapons.*
- *There is a nuclear arms race on, a war on and an election on.*
- *In this context, you do not want an extremist president.*

The logic is stark and the dramatization of that logic is even more so. To characterize your opponent's policies as 'to go into the dark' was quite a claim, but it made the choice between the two candidates into one of historical importance. By doing so, it involved the viewer. On the other hand, the logic of 'Cliff top' went more like this:

- *We badly need to make the Labour Party more glamorous.*
- *Let's hire a commercials director.*

The only logic is tied to how the party wanted to appear, not why the viewer should vote for them.

The point is that television is the most powerful weapon in the advertiser's armoury, so it's a shame to waste it on mediocrity.

RULE EIGHT:
BE AMBITIOUS

Joy equals talent plus skill.

Judy Delton, 1990

The last two chapters have invited you to be brutally honest in your pursuit of simple communication and in understanding the nature of various media. Both ask that you supplant your lay view of advertising (if that's what you have) with a professional one. The conventional way to do this is through experience. The way to get experience is to get a job in advertising and hang around in it long enough. Sadly, you can't expect to do that. You need to start producing work of quality on day one. To do that you have to want to very much, which is why I have included this chapter.

If you see a brief or project as being a minor thing not worthy of your attention, or not worthy of the full treatment, of all the research and hours of re-writes, it self-evidently ends up a minor piece of work.

You'll be amazed how good even the most boring project can turn out. My favourite example is the station idents that were introduced in the early 1990s for BBC2.

Before these were produced, this might have been an uninspiring job. After all, how many different ways can you write '2' on a screen for five seconds? One D&AD gold pencil later, imagine getting the brief for a new batch. Suddenly it's an

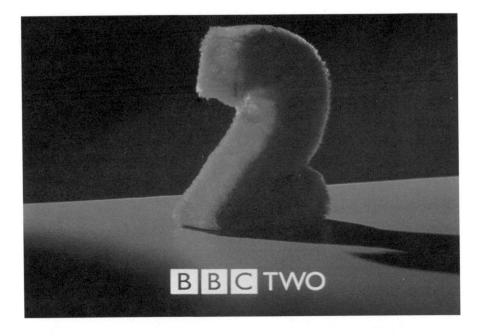

enviable one. Just think how many different ways that you can write '2' on a screen for five seconds. Nothing has changed but the understanding of the possibilities.

The moral is: don't envisage things turning out dull and boring. Imagine a strange future world where car stickers change governments. Improve your own standards by competing with rival writers in your office, with the work of the best in the industry, or with yourself.

When you've done something good, stop feeling proud and ask yourself if it's better than the best around. Good ideas are usually produced between people, so work with others. If you can't create with someone, at least bounce your idea off others. Don't get annoyed with them if they don't react as you want them to. If their faces don't actually light up with joy and comprehension, you perhaps haven't produced the best possible.

Maybe it isn't possible to be the best within the restrictions of the brief. So redefine the brief in your head so the restrictions give you some sort of new idea of what the best could be.

Don't expect miracles. Rarely are first ideas the best. If you're uncertain about an idea, leave it overnight and see what you think when you come to it fresh. If you're still uncertain in the morning, it's probably not so good.

It's amazing how dumb a great line can become between 6 o'clock in the evening and 9 o'clock the following morning.

Mike Lescarbeau

In the meantime, write more. It will be obvious when you've found a good idea from the reactions of others. Your own worst enemy will tell you it's good and will be more miserable than you could ever have wished. The right idea is irresistible.

It's worth it. If you spend 40 hours producing hundreds of ideas, another 40 hours crafting and honing the one best idea, the fact that the end product is brilliant is no surprise to you, but to others it seems to have just popped out of your head. People will say you're a genius. There's no point telling them you're not because they won't believe you.

END OF RESTRICTIONS

Rules only work well as a structure where the motivation is to halt something. This is ideal for advertising as so much of it very nearly qualifies as environmental pollution. If the majority of advertising were at least clear and simple, no one would complain. After all, no one seems to be bothered by road signs, yet they convey all kinds of information on a vast scale, and do so with utmost clarity. Many of the ads I have championed in this book, such as *The Economist* campaign, have something of the road sign about them. However, while calling a halt works fine at road junctions, it works badly when encouraging an agency, a creative team or one's own department to solve complex problems with a brilliant idea. If you want one of those, a suggestion has already been made in the introduction to this book, namely to allow time.

IDEAS ON IDEAS

Further guidance on ideas is less straightforward. It might seem idiotic to attempt to instruct another person how to have ideas. The surest advice would be simply to get to work. Start on your research, ponder practical things such as media, start writing dull, longwinded headlines that are little more than a précis of the briefing material and wait for that miracle that is the aptitude of the human mind to make problem-solving leaps of logic. Just as sure is the advice that when you feel you've hit a brick wall, stop and do something different, ideally elsewhere.

Some writers on this subject recommend that one thing you can do to improve your ability to have fresher ideas is to get out more, to watch films, look at art, visit all kinds of stimulating cultural phenomena in order to feed the brain. This is good advice, in that it contributes to your general stock of influences.

I can recommend the opening chapter of *Screenwriting for Narrative Film and Television* by William Miller, which gives a nice description of how to regard your own brain and what to expect of it. I particularly liked the understanding of the 'incubation' period of the creative process where the creative person in question appears to be completely idle, not involved at all with work but occupied with mindless pastimes. This not only put me at ease about my own inexplicable interest in pin-ball and mah jong during what were supposed to be busy periods, but is also reassuring to all those who suffer blocks or doubts about their ability.

There are other techniques for having ideas. Sometimes the very act of reducing unnecessary detail creates the idea.

Sometimes creativity is no more than problem solving. But in a way it's good that some part of the process of having ideas is inscrutable. On occasions, I've been asked how an idea was arrived at and invariably the only true answer is that I or someone else had simply said out of the blue, 'Why don't we do x?'

Below are four examples of ads with unpromising subject matter whose authors were clearly harbouring more than average ambition.

BE ORIGINAL

Beyond this, I do have one thought to add on the subject of ideas and it comes in the phrase I used earlier, 'It might seem idiotic... .'

Many ideas that end up catching the imagination, and from history, many ideas that end up changing the world, start from a moment of apparent idiocy or a naïve suggestion.

By their very nature such ideas are original. For some time I considered the inclusion in this book of a rule 9 along the lines of 'Be original'. But it may not have escaped your notice that advertising occasionally steals ideas from films, art, TV programmes and other fields of creative endeavour. The annoying thing if you have noticed the phenomenon is that many of the ads which steal ideas can be very successful, or very enjoyable, or both. It is usually unfair to accuse people who do this of plagiarism where it is clearly the intelligent use of cultural references. And where the resultant ads are badly realized, then that is what is wrong, not the fact that they've used an existing technique or set of characters without attributing the source.

Part of the job of advertising is to make a link between the advertiser and the consumer. You may recall the two blobs and the X used earlier. Any rule that decrees that everything should be original would wipe out a lot of good stuff that relates easily to its audience. Nevertheless, just because it can't be enshrined as a

"*I just give the people what they want. Phenomenal cow sex at a fair price.*"

Judy's Cow Breeding Services
(206) 263-3938

rule, doesn't make originality wrong. Much as I defend the apt appropriation of an existing idea, I ultimately prefer originality.

The reason isn't anything to do with artistic integrity, but longevity. In *The Western Canon*, Harold Bloom wrote, 'one mark of originality that can win canonical status for a literary work is a strangeness that we either never altogether assimilate, or becomes such a given that we are blinded to its idiosyncrasies'. This is an insight about the world's greatest literature that he will not thank me for applying to the grubby world of advertising, but the point is such a good one that I can't resist. He's saying that great literary works often create something so strange that instead of rejecting them, we do the opposite and suddenly feel that we can't imagine life without them. They are both strange and commonplace at the same time.

This trait is, if anything, a more observable one in advertising. Commercials stick around in the memory sometimes out of pure oddness. The Peugeot commercial from several years back where a car drove along a country road while an adjacent field of sugar cane was burnt down for no reason was so strange, so inscrutable that it just sits there in the memory and refuses to go away. This is another area where the advocates of USP (unique selling position) advertising, those that insist on a strict flow chart of communication, from promise to benefit, seem short of answers. They can either try to fit the commercial to their own theory or simply say it isn't really advertising at all. When Benetton ran their remarkable series of posters showing shocking visuals of dying HIV patients and copulating horses, the marketing gurus and theoreticians couldn't really account for its success, so they just didn't use it as an example in their books. The launch of First Direct telephone banking was similarly dismissed as having nothing to do with advertising. One poster showed a pair of Wellington boots standing by the door... and nothing else. Another showed a small patch of grass... and nothing else. If these posters had nothing to do with advertising, why was the launch such a palpable success? How do you account for the success of such horrors as the Ferrero Rocher ads, where the guests at an Ambassador's party treat the arrival of a plate of chocolates with a bizarre reverence usually reserved for popes? The answer is in that word, 'bizarre'. Of course, there is plenty of logic to be found in all the above examples. But you can attach logic to anything. There are limitless ways to advertise a product and some strand of logic or other can justify them all. If I wanted to advertise the Samaritans by showing a tap-dancing moose you could justify everything that's wrong about it as being what's right about it. And vice versa.

It has been said that if, as a client, you are scared to run an ad, then it's a good sign and you should run it. Perhaps the above examples show why. Steve Henry, who I quoted right at the very beginning of this book, allegedly used a similar method when hiring staff. If, while looking through a creative team's portfolio he didn't know whether he liked the ideas or not, he reasoned that it was because the work was outside his experience and way of perceiving ads. So he hired the team.

Originality is one of the most identifiable characteristics of memorable ads, but at the same time the very word 'copywriting' reminds us that at the very heart of advertising is the concept of reiteration. You may have heard the phrase, 'repetition is reputation'. The whole idea of a campaign is to maintain a thought and a tone from previous advertising. If your product is cheap to produce and you're selling it as a luxury item (diamonds spring to mind) you will not be looking to change much about the advertising that got you in that position. 'Rule 9: Be original' would not merely be controversial; it would, sadly, be wrong. What I would suggest, though, is to avoid the unoriginal execution. For example:

- *Commercials that take place in lifts. Why do people keep doing this? Perhaps because a lift journey lasts approximately 30 seconds and is therefore an ideal place to show someone enjoying a chocolate bar or* ice cream in a certain orgasmic fashion that is another over-familiar advertising device. Whatever the reason, we've all seen it now.

- Press/posters that feature cuckoo clocks. It may be a hilarious place to show a product, dangling on the end of an extending cuckoo support, but again, we've seen it now, thank you.
- Two women speaking in a kitchen. Or two teenagers discussing spots in a bathroom. I suspect that these executional scenarios will still be with us in a thousand years. However, where we aren't specifically briefed to set ads in these locations, we can all help by not doing so of our own free wills.
- Engineer's voice interrupting a radio ad. Just because it's post-modern doesn't mean it hasn't been done.
- Headlines for cars that mention head and heart. David Abbot's version was, 'Dear Head. Couldn't agree more. Regards, Heart.' Surely that should bring an end to this headline genus.
- 'When it comes to' at the start of copy, and 'So...' starting the last or penultimate line of copy. This is a very tired way to write copy. It may make life easier for the writer to use these conventional lead-ins and wind-ups, but in a piece of sales material they read like Jack Lemmon in 'Glengarry Glen Ross'.
- Reindeer in Christmas ads. Being a creative means you should be able to think of 100 uses of a brick. The same applies to briefs that seem to have no great creative opportunities, such as Christmas ads. I'm sure you can add a few more Christmas perennials yourself. Have faith. There are more Christmas ideas out there waiting to be found.
- Man throwing sticks for a dog. Seen it. This falls into a category that Denis Norden might call, 'Promising situations for mirthful conclusions' or some such thing. I would add situations such as desert islands, doctors' waiting rooms, men carrying a pane of glass across a road and queues at bus stops. There are many more. Even if they haven't been used in ads before, people have seen these so-called comic situations in sketches, sitcoms and magazine cartoons, so they will still look tired.

■ *Puns on 'interest' in financial ads. Tempting, I know. If you'll forgive the pun, there is very little purchase to be found for pleasant witticisms in the world of financial mechanisms. But originality is still desirable.*

■ *Busy mums. As with other stereotypes, they're best avoided.*

■ *Cartoon rabbits, chickens. Animation does not guarantee originality. In certain product categories it is the norm. What is original is to use a cartoon to advertise in a product category where animation hasn't been used in living memory. Such categories are fast disappearing.*

■ *Mirrors. Every couple of months someone produces an ad that uses a mirror surface to reflect, supposedly, the viewer, with a line like, 'Are you looking at someone who needs a personal pension?' Not only has this idea been done many, many times, it can also be seen from those previous examples that it doesn't actually work.*

Of course, this list is regularly traduced by someone producing good work in one of these categories. There's always another great animated animal just around the corner, another new joke that starts, 'A man walked into a pub,' so don't take it too seriously.

CONCLUSION

An expensive ad represents the toil, attention, testing, wit, art and skill of many people.

Marshall McLuhan, *Understanding Media*, 1964

If you have a busy job in a marketing department you may have opened this book in order to find out how to sharpen up your own words, how to judge the work of your department and perhaps to help manage your company's brand through its advertising. The internal and external communications of a company define its identity and if they follow the rules, especially that of simplicity, it makes it easy for everyone in that company to live the brand.

Having read the book you might well decide that regardless of the rules there is one principle behind them: to write properly requires far more application than seems necessary at first sight. The idea of researching something that appears only a few times before disappearing forever may seem pointless. The idea of rewriting something over and over, even the very notion of stopping in mid flow to spend 10 seconds trying to find a better word may seem wasteful. That's because it is. Waste, in copywriting, is a fuel.

This is even more the case when coming up with advertising ideas. When friends tell me they like an ad of mine, they seem to think I'm a very clever person. If, in conversation later, I let drop that I wrote over a hundred scripts for a particular brief, with every word and visual carefully thought out, they look at me with something approaching disgust. The investment of time and creative effort in something so transient seems imbecilic. It works the same way for conjurors. It's easier to shrug in mystification than to believe a performer would bother hiring an accomplice and sit him or her in an auditorium for a whole evening simply so that person can pick a prearranged card at a prearranged time. The bother isn't worth the effect for one person, but it's worth it for the 200 other mystified souls, calculates the conjuror. This is a calculation you too need to make. If you wish to produce your own advertising yourself, you either have to accept that you may not be able to devote yourself to achieving the full potential of the brand or company concerned, or that you will have to devote yourself to little else. If you don't fancy either, you can always use a freelance copywriter.

USING FREELANCE COPYWRITERS

One thing you lose when using a single freelance copywriter rather than an agency's or someone in your own company, is the invisible input of other people. Freelances tend to work in isolation – great for writing a novel, not great for writing material that is intended for instant, mass communication. If one were to trace the progress of a piece of work through an agency, client company and any other group of people with which it comes into contact, you'd be surprised how much it gradually mutates between its inception and its realization. Whether it improves or gets worse depends on the quality and talent of all those people, but when the intra and inter company relations work well, the end product is blown clean by the attention and criticism it attracts. It is this that polishes your finished article as much as your own private exertions.

There is a collegiate effect that comes into play when producing an ad or any creative product that isn't a personal work of art. This includes suggestions by well-meaning or well-informed colleagues, but also points of fact, problems of lack of originality or unintentional plagiarism, of lapses into irrelevance or subjectivity. The constant, informal airing of the work in front of peers, clients, production and traffic personnel, wives and husbands, even reps and air conditioning engineers, can contribute in some way to the honing and sharpening of a product. Fans of the film 'Casablanca' might like to try to find out a single author for the finished movie. It seems to have been produced by a sequence of random events and people who inhabited the brilliant machine of that particular Hollywood studio during that era.

Your freelance copywriter may do everything he or she should. The person may be a genius in the truest possible sense. Yet few world-changing events are credited to freelance individuals working alone. For acknowledged geniuses of advertising it's often an unfaceable truth that their best work was produced in a highly unsatisfactory arrangement where they couldn't get their own way, and couldn't bash it all out in one meeting with the client.

If there is no struggle there is no progress.
Fredrick Douglas, *Narrative of His Life*

It may be interesting at this point to stop reading for a moment and think of an idea that has recently changed things in your company. A new product, a new advertising idea, a new departmental innovation, a new promotional idea. Use your memory and work backwards. Where did that idea spring from? Come to think of it, wasn't it something a secretary said after seeing the rejected boards after a meeting that somebody jokingly mentioned to the finance director in the toilet?

Maybe not, in your case. But the interplay of personnel, the egos and relationships in companies surely rings bells, more so, at any rate, than a scenario in which the idea landed complete on your desk in exchange for a cheque. One of my earliest experiences in advertising was walking into the agency early one morning, a day or two after a Van Gogh Sunflowers painting sold at auction for a record figure. Someone from a department I didn't know existed had pinned up a clipping from the newspaper with a tub of Flora Margarine crudely drawn in. Flora margarine was a sunflower margarine we advertised at the time. 'This could be an ad' I pointed out, and 48 hours later an artist had repainted Van Gogh's Sunflowers with a tub of Flora Margarine mysteriously appearing in the composition. This painting was then photographed hanging on a living room wall and published with the line, 'Very tasty if you've got the bread', a tabloidy pun that I'm not sure stands the test of time. The following day the ad was in the press. The week after, someone handed me a copy of a US arts newspaper that had discovered the ad and published it on their back page, so taken were they with the image.

There's much misattribution of ideas in advertising, and many people lose a lot of sleep about people taking credit for their ideas. This is unfortunate, but inevitable. A cynical person will shrug and recall the phrase, 'Everybody's job is to make their boss look good' and hope one day that the food chain operates in their favour. The non-cynic will accept that ideas and politics should be kept apart because ideas really do happen between people. This is visible in the organization of creative departments into teams, which can be competitive, but usually cooperative. The person who put the Sunflowers ad in my head wasn't even in the building at the time his idea took root. I will never, as they say, have a chance to thank him. What's more, I will never know what tiny remark or circumstance prompted him to leave his newspaper clipping around. But it just proves that ideas are born and evolve within a dynamic. The egos, the financial limitations, the boss's spouse (a character passed down in agency mythology) – all these may at times seem to be against the development of ideas, but in fact they are a relevant part of that dynamic.

This isn't really meant to be an anti-freelance message, more a suggestion not to use them just for a quiet life, or for the organizational simplicity of working with them. There are no doubt situations where great work isn't needed. There are situations all creatives will recognize where despite the radiant positivity of a briefing, what is really required is 'cannon fodder'. Cannon fodder means creative work produced for a meeting in order for that meeting to have something to talk about, overlooking the fact that there are no pressing advertising deadlines.

As some of my best friends work freelance, presumably including at some point in the future, myself, I can't recommend you blank that part of the copywriting industry. But if you do use freelances with a genuine interest in producing a good end product, work with them as you would an agency, and include them in meetings and get-togethers of those who work on the account, then feed the product back to them as it's produced. If nothing else, it's a waste of most freelances' talents to use them simply as a producer of the initial creative work.

One thing you notice about the best creative teams is not so much the brilliance of their work at source, but how they stay in touch with it, constantly searching for the perfect expression and execution of their idea and how deftly they respond when changes need to be made. The traditional creative response to changing an original thought has been not to, as in the joke, 'How many creatives does it take change a light bulb? We're not changing it.' In reality, few creatives benefit from the overuse of this mantra. Instead, I recommend the principle, 'Only improve' when faced with mandatory changes. This often requires a truly creative approach as well as real experience and skill. Your pet freelance, the man or woman who moseys in from the Home Counties, is perhaps more valuable than you realize. But you can only benefit from the greater part of their talent if they are involved fully with the thinking before and the development after the initial creative work is produced, as well as with the other personnel involved in your project.

THE POWER OF WORDS

A decade ago this book was but a deck of slides, a presentation in preparation for the BBC. Its existence was the result of a curious situation that had occurred in that august corporation. The BBC was and is a unique phenomenon, the original public service broadcaster, paid for by a licence fee, not advertising.

An advertising professional might produce an interesting cultural by-product, but in the BBC's eyes, he or she was a half-formed creature born out of bad schooling and low commerce, an idiot savant with a line of patter and the brassy self-confidence to foist ideas on clients. In contrast, the people of the BBC lived on a privileged Laputa, an elevated island of cultural sophistication, far from the depravities of commercial necessity.

The only mild threat to this sunlit world was the requirement for the BBC's charter to be renewed every six years or so by the government of the day, but for such a powerful, well connected and popular establishment this was normally an easy negotiation. That is, until about 10 years ago, when the Conservative Government believed organizations should be sculpted by the fierce economic winds of the market. They were no respecters of institutional sacred cows, which were sent to the slaughterhouse in a series of successful privatizations. A chill wind passed through the ivory towers of the BBC as the next charter renewal came into view. For the first time the BBC was truly in danger of losing its position. Laputians stirred uneasily in their gilded chambers, talked nervously around the water coolers in their dappled groves. We must keep the licence fee? We must resist pressure to join the commercial world? We need to win support from the public at large. But how to put our case?

Surely not, we couldn't, could we?

But what else is there?

So it was that the BBC approached advertising agencies to create popular support for their status quo, through a series of promotional films, effectively commercials in the usual slots between programmes, celebrating the good works of the organization – the drama, comedy, natural history and children's programmes for which the BBC is a beacon of excellence.

As it happened, though I did work on the resulting campaign of promotional films at the agency for which I then toiled, the resources the BBC had already were those that made the most difference. They had legions of competent writers and filmmakers, what they had lacked was a reason to use them on anything other than the programmes themselves. Quite right too, you would think. Licence fee payers would rather their yearly contribution be spent on a bodice in a costume drama over a continuity announcer's studio fee. However, without realizing it, that same licence fee payer's opinion of the BBC was formed by those very voices. To illustrate the point, think of a radio station and tell me that its character isn't that of the voices between the records rather than the records themselves. Remember, an organization cannot decide not to have a tone of voice. You might think that the BBC's future would be decided by the quality of its programming rather than its tone of voice. In an ideal world, perhaps. But in the real world what comprised a good programme was decided by a variety of opinions and agendas. Was it the adaptation of a classic novel, the programme with highest foreign sales, or the one with the largest audience? In a commercial organization it would be simpler to define success, but at the BBC it was impossible to show its audience figures to substantiate its existence, as it could be pointed out that these were inappropriately high for a public service broadcaster, whose charter indicated that its job was to inform, educate and entertain. The BBC had to convince the nation that it was a vigorous, tightly run, well managed, force for good in the broadcasting firmament. Though self-promotion did have a positive effect to some, who liked to see this then lumbering, shapeless British institution stick up for itself, it also irritated others.

Advertising can often be used as a blunt instrument; a good example is, funnily enough, during privatization situations, or launches of products, when the goal is to bludgeon your way into public consciousness without worrying too much about the long-term consequences. Though the BBC's self-promotion campaign did its fair share of bludgeoning, it quickly realized that this was not the long-term solution. By interacting with advertising agencies it came to the realization that its tone of voice mattered. This is evidenced in that innocent phrase 'continuity announcer', the voice that links one programme to the next. That voice is the organization's continuous contact with the public. In a context where programming is as disparate as it is at the BBC, those messages, trailers, links, apologies, promotions, addresses to write to and so on, told the viewer everything they needed to know about the organization. Before the corporate communications campaign started, that voice was lofty and presumptuous. It would list the entire evening's viewing, reading from a list on a screen, rather like a teacher naming the lakes of Africa or presenting the chronology of the discovery of subatomic particles. We were presumably expected to write these down, as if there were no other option but to watch each one and construct our lives around them. Alternatively, we might be forced to watch, for the fourth time that evening, a badly made trailer promoting a forthcoming programme. As the BBC didn't have to pay for this time on its own channel, it would not be constrained in time length. What on other channels would be the most expensive prime time slot was filled with dull panning shots over fields while a long drawn out voiceover described nothing of much interest. Anyone having the cheek to channel hop would have been able to compare this apparently slack-minded, inward looking organization with a vibrant, fast-moving environment on commercial channels, where every second (of your time) was precious.

By communing with the enemy in the shape of advertising agencies and research groups the BBC realized how its own corporate voice sounded to others, and like most people when they hear their own voice for the first time, they didn't much like it.

I continued to work with the BBC, occasionally holding seminars for the staff involved in writing trailers and continuity announcements. In doing so I was hoping to pass on some of the intensity, rigour and even passion attached to the bits between programmes by those for whom the bits between programmes is all they have. I quickly realized that the goal was to create the sense of a market for excellence, where there was a real feeling of pressure, to force those charged with the job of writing, to spend longer on it, expect more from it. The most essential property of the trailers and promotions was that they should prove the case for watching the BBC over other channels and the case for the licence fee. In short they had to entertain. If a programme needed to be trailed it had to measure up to the task. If a promotion wanted to be on screen for 60 seconds at prime time, it had to be the most entertaining thing on the box for that 60 seconds anywhere in Western Europe. With the talent at their disposal they were well placed to convert this principle into some astonishingly watchable films. A cover version of Lou Reed's 'Perfect Day', with each line sung by a different singing star with a different style to convey the variety of BBC Radio output was not just more entertaining than a monotonous continuity announcer's version, but infinitely more eloquent and effective.

What this case study illustrates is that powerful communication arises from context. Winston Churchill's speeches somehow rose to the occasion of impending invasion but would have been inappropriate asking for a packet of mints.

The power of words in any situation is only partly to do with their content. Why do you open your boss's e-mail before the one from the nonentity in the administration department? Why read the newspapers more thoroughly after a major news event? The importance of certain pieces of writing often coincides with the fact that it is more powerfully written. But of course it is no coincidence that your Global Chairman's e-mail carries with it a certain attitude, self-regard or potency than that of the nonentity, even if that nonentity turns out to be the better writer. The authors know what is expected of them ahead of time and know that they are required to rise to the occasion as appropriate. The boss's choice of style is based on the fact that he needs to maintain the appearance his managerial role has hitherto established. The journalist writing the report of the cataclysm or the fight of the century knows he or she cannot simply narrate the tale of its happening in the same style of his or her letters to the regional gas supplier. The more earth-shattering the event the more likely he or she is to choose powerful constructions that do it justice.

So far, so obvious. But the writer of an ad must take one step further. They must think a little more like Citizen Kane, for whom the importance of a story is down to the proprietor. Any story phrased correctly could be a front page splash. You have to imagine the context where the message is important, then create through the language and imagery at your disposal.

Having played the Citizen Kane role for an agency, the Creative Director, I have witnessed the remarkable transformation that takes place as you go through a sequence of reviews of creative work. The brief is seen first, and signed if it is cogent and presents a reasonable attempt at a simple proposition. The first stage of creative work you see is of a certain standard and generally reflects the assumptions you made on seeing the brief. The second edges towards something a little in advance of the first, predictably. Then things can start to take off. As you turn down work for the many reasons for which it is possible to reject work, not only do the possibilities of the brief start to improve, but you also become aware that the brief itself is starting to appear more important. The project on which the company is embarking, whether it's the launch of a new car or a 3p mobile phone tariff, becomes increasingly significant.

Sometimes it is relatively easy to make a brief or a product seem more important. A sun cream sold as a tanning aid can also be sold as a barrier against skin cancer. A mint sold as a mouth freshener can also be sold as a way to get closer to the opposite sex. Or as the BBC found, a bland corporate message about the breadth of radio coverage in the even blander context of a corporate financing review can also be a life-enhancing celebration of music. The lyrics to 'Perfect Day' were changed by the context in which they were used, an effect seen in all the best advertising. The words on the *Economist* ads you see in this and almost every advertising book are empowered by the competitive business context that informs them and in which they are seen. Simple words given powerful frames.

It doesn't sound much, but it's all you need.

EXAMPLES

Logic and over-analysis can immobilize and sterilize an idea. It's like love – the more you analyze it, the faster it disappears.

Bill Bernbach

The decent thing to do now is to finish with a collection of good advertisements. This is harder to do than it seems, as people tend to assess advertising according to different criteria. If a campaign does the trick in raising awareness and selling the product, many would be happy with that. The idea that 'good advertising' should relate to anything other than sales can infuriate some people, but if, instead of the terms 'good' and 'bad', the terms 'long term' and 'short term' were used, many would change their positions.

There is no obvious reason why an ad should last longer than the weeks or months after it is seen. There are few things more sobering than to look at an old copy of *Campaign* or *Marketing* from a year or two ago and see the campaigns launched with high hopes that have all but vanished from collective memory. The only place their impact is still felt is in the meetings between the clients and agencies responsible. It is unarguably good news, then, if a particular line or idea seems to hang around in the memory. I have my own theory that some great brands and businesses are built from single, great ads. The public obstinately remembers certain chocolate bars, margarines, makes of condoms or even cars, from one particular commercial, sometimes in the distant past. The entire reputation of a brand or a company can be based on one remembered line or action in that commercial.

People can still replay these lines or actions decades afterwards, irrespective of the ructions their advertising departments may have endured in the intervening years. These great ads aren't always great in the creative sense either. Or rather they are, but not in the award-winning creative sense. What they do tend to do is break moulds.

Then again, some great ads don't break moulds. Some brands like Volkswagen and *The Economist* just do an ordinary, everyday advertising job with extraordinary skill. In the absence of a formula, then, a definition of good advertising might be helpful.

GOOD ADVERTISING

'Good' is one of those words like 'large', 'clean' and 'edible' that people use without realizing that it may mean something completely different to the person they're saying it to. For Adrian Holmes, copywriter and former chairman of Lowe Howard-Spink, 'good' was 'the enemy of great'. This is one of advertising's better utterances. I'm convinced there is a part of the brain that releases endorphins every time you have an idea. The result is that you get a buzz of pleasure identical to the one you experience when completing a jigsaw or answering a crossword clue. This Pavlovian response militates against human beings being good at writing ads. A jigsaw or crossword can be declared finished, but when writing ads it's up to you to say when you're finished and it is critical that you don't declare the job finished too early. The same applies to a press release or a speech. Just because it looks like the right length and covers the right information, does that make it finished? For that you need to engage your judgement.

It used to be that an ad was good if it simply communicated a selling message or a unique selling position (USP). It still is for many people in advertising and marketing. But to leave it at that is to ignore the fact that in today's media there are many non-selling messages being carried. Even putting aside public information work that involves a different kind of sell, there's plenty of corporate advertising that seems to be intended only to announce the organization's name in a positive way or spread good cheer among its shareholders. Saying 'Hi' is now a USP.

Dave Dye wrote and art-directed the ad below, showing an ordinary street along which lines of copy were spaced out at regular intervals along the pavement. The first says 'Just to the signpost.' Then, at the signpost, comes the line 'Just to the car.' At the car is the line 'Just to the crossroads' and so on. Anyone who runs will recognize this mental state and this makes the ad actually enjoyable. How it does a job of selling is difficult to articulate. Does the smell of chlorine make you want to swim or the sound of someone shouting 'Send it long' make you want to play football? If so, then that is the way it works. This may be the meaning of the US phrase 'Sell the sizzle not the steak', though I'd be lying if I said I was certain.

Regardless of what sales gurus might say, if you have a relatively straightforward product such as a training shoe or a stock cube and wish to support it with regular advertising, there are only so many things you can say. How good does stitching have to be to bear this kind of scrutiny? Do you really want to know what's in those hard, brown cubes of odoriferous grit?

The fact is, there does occasionally seem to exist an alternative advertising universe untouched by the US sales gurus with their marketing formulae such as USPs and AIDA (Attract, Inform, create Desire, call to Action). Nike ads seem to hang out there, identifying the consumer by seeming to enjoy the same things. Some may protest that there is a USP detectable. Those fundamentalists who can't bring themselves to call an ad good unless it has a USP will, if they like the ad, see one in it. But, for me, if you can't play the proposition back within a moment or two, surely it isn't really there and the fact that you like it can be put down to something personal. It speaks to you.

So, 'good advertising' means neither commercially successful, though that is a part of it, nor brilliantly put together, though that is part of it too. A good ad is one that goes far beyond the default ad, the ad that merely answers a brief. It makes something of it that lingers after its burst of appearances. Something that combines good thinking and brilliant creative realization. It almost always needs a USP. What is crucial in every case is an advertising idea. But you are the final judge. Take every chance to nurture your judgement and develop it by observing the advertising around you. In the words of James Lowther, a writer with a long association with the Saatchis, 'The best copywriters are not always the ones with the highest ability but the ones with the highest standards.'

Leaded petrol causes brain damage.

Which may explain why some people are still using it.

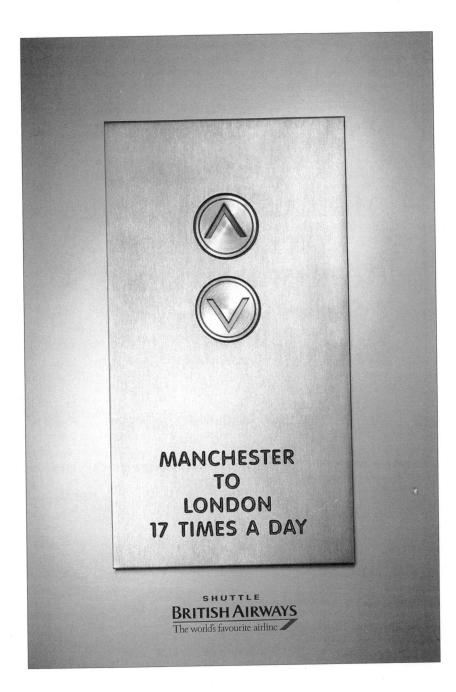

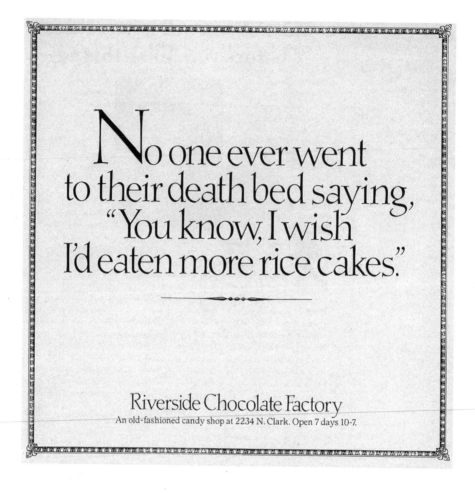

THE NEW PEUGEOT 206 GTI

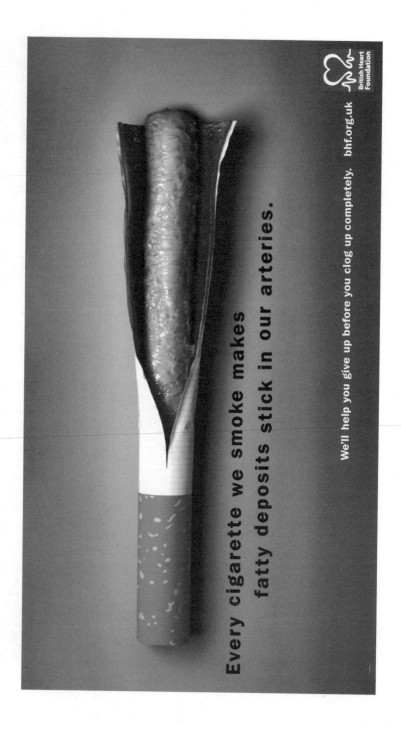

Pilsner
Urquell
Czech the
Original
When beer foams,
ditty is not far.
"We brew the Pilsner Urquell by day.
At night we drink Pilsner
Urquell too."
We sing many such loud drinking songs of Czech country for we brew the first golden one in Pilsen here.
"Czech girl have
Czech beer drink
Oh, such pleasures
Only Czechs have."
Numerously we sing, because the work is over, and we are glad to see Mr Snabl, the brewmeister come, despite he's foul spawn of devil to work for.
Then we mouth the glorious proverbs.
"Good beer can also be in ugly barrel."
"Tankard, tankard,
I know love to you."
"Beautify the mother who gives birth to the malterer."
"When beer foams, ditty is not far."
- which last one is most true when we drink Pilsner Urquell.
Please sing them too.
Pilsner
Urquell.
Czech the
Original.
Mr. Snabl

PEUGEOT 206 GTi. ABNORMAL POWER.
0-60mph in 7.1 sec. 'The greatest GTi of all time' (Auto Express).

PEUGEOT

FURTHER READING

I recommend Alister Crompton, *The Craft of Copywriting* (Random House, 1979, London). The writing is of a kind normally referred to as limpid, the description of how an agency works as an organization is also excellent. Having worked in agencies for many years, it was a relief to have the mechanisms, departments and delicate power structures made clear to me for the first time. Even the uncodified power relationships such as that between creatives and traffic men, on whom they rely for laminated proofs, are elucidated for the benefit of all. It has lasted well but inevitably has grown out of date in places. Copywriters of Compton's not-so-distant generation tended to rely on a certain charm for a very good reason. Advertising at that time was regarded as an uninvited visitor. Anyone who blundered into your home claiming how good his or her company's product was would receive not so much a 'How much is it?' as a 'Get out of my home'. Today, the consumer's response is more likely to be a weary 'I've been expecting you, you might as well come in'.

In years to come it may well seem quaint to even discuss mass communication at all when direct-mail companies get together with digital technology and advertise to everyone individually. According to Greg Dyke, once Director-General of the BBC, mass communication may turn out to be a blip in history. He was talking of the growth of subscription television in the United States, where people can choose and pay directly for just those channels they want to watch. And where TV goes, the advertisers follow.

One book that will take a long while to become out of date is *Hey Whipple, Squeeze This* (John Wiley & Sons, 1998, New York). It's a personal account of working in advertising agencies in the United States, writing great ads and winning awards. Highlights include his fellow copywriter who was nicknamed 'Win a boat' because he wrote an ad with the headline 'Win a boat'. Cruel, but fair.

David Ogilvy's *Confessions of an Advertising Man* (Atheneum, 1963, New York) is a worthwhile read from many standpoints. It is interesting that the 'man in the eye patch' campaign for Hathaway shirts that he describes in the book seemed woefully out of date in its thinking when I first read of it around 15 years ago. Nowadays, this piece of intentional daftness smacks of modernity.

There are some beautifully produced books published by D&AD, not the least of which is their annual, which showcases the best ads of the year as assessed by formidable panels of judges. There is also *The Copywriting Book* (RotoVision, 1995, Switzerland) which simply names some of the world's best copy-writers, and gives them a couple of pages to describe their approach. Apart from some nice tips, the book is valuable for allowing you to read in one place the work of some fine writers for once not having to harness their skills to a particular product. The best of these articles, and possibly the only one that persuades you to take up copywriting right away, is that of Neil French who recommends you start any piece of copy by choosing a good bottle of Rioja and taking out the cork. There are also the equivalent publications by the US awards organizations, in particular The One Club, and their annual, *The One Show* (RotoVision, Switzerland).

Those works that set out to be instructive rather than illustrative seem to focus on direct mail and promotional litera-ture copy to the exclusion of posters, TV and so on. This is under-standable in so far as most marketing people tend to delegate to agencies or freelancers these more intense reaches of copywriting. Of these, James Essinger, *How To Write Marketing Copy That Gets Results* (Pitman Publishing, 1996, London), is an excellent presentation of general writing techniques and only the highest of morals prevented me from extravagant plagiarism. Beyond these, I would recommend H W Fowler, *Modern English Usage* (Oxford University Press, 1926, Oxford).

Already mentioned in the text are: Tony Antin *Great Print Advertising* (John Wiley & Sons, 1993, New York), Wolff Olins *Guide to Corporate Identity* (The Design Council, 1990, London), Larry Dobrow *When Advertising Tried Harder* (Friendly Press, 1984, New York), Eugen Herrigel *Zen in the Art of Archery* (Penguin Arkana, 1999, London), William Miller *Screenwriting for Narrative, Film and Television* (Columbus Books, 1988, London) and Harold Bloom *The Western Canon* (Harcourt Brace & Co, 1994, New York). Material from the 'Daisy' case study may be found in Barry Goldwater and Jack Casserly, *Goldwater* (Doubleday, 1988, London) and *Vietnam: A Television History* produced for public television by WGBH Boston in cooperation with Central Independent Television/United Kingdom and Antenne-2/France and in association with LRE Productions.

INDEX

Page numbers in *italic* indicate examples